RECLAIMING THE LOST LEGACY

The Founders and
The First Amendment

RECLAIMING THE LOST LEGACY

The Founders and The First Amendment

with Introduction by

D. James Kennedy

CORAL RIDGE MINISTRIES
Fort Lauderdale

Reclaiming The Lost Legacy: The Founders and The First Amendment

Front Cover Images, left to right
George Washington by Gilbert Stuart © Museum of the City of New York/CORBIS
Portrait of Thomas Jefferson by Gilbert Stuart © Burstein Collection/CORBIS
Painted Portrait Of James Madison © Bettmann/CORBIS

Back Cover Image
The Signing of the Constitution in 1787. Undated painting by Stearns. © Bettmann/CORBIS

Coral Ridge Ministries
P.O. Box 40
Fort Lauderdale, Florida 33302

Printed in the United States of America

RECLAIMING THE LOST LEGACY
The Founders and The First Amendment

Table of Contents

INTRODUCTION

T he Library of Congress is home to an exhibition so profound and revealing that it is unlikely to be found in the library of any modern American public school. Called "Religion and the Founding of the American Republic," this exhibit offers a clear historical look at the impact of the Christian religion on public life.

When I came upon this exhibit a few years ago, during a visit to our nation's capital, I was particularly surprised to find a formal acknowledgment of history that is conveniently left out of so many revisionist versions of our American heritage. Most striking, however, was the real story behind the oft-quoted declaration of a "separation of church and state" attributed to Thomas Jefferson.

During the second year of his first administration, Jefferson wrote to the Danbury Baptist Association, assuring these Connecticut faithful that the government would not interfere with their churches and the free exercise of their devotion to God. These were more than mere words. President Jefferson put this commitment into action only two days later when he began to attend the services of a church that happened to be the largest congregation in America at that time.

Even more fascinating is the fact that the church Jefferson attended just two days after he wrote the Danbury letter was meeting in the chambers of the House of Representatives! Thomas Jefferson went to church in the U.S. Capitol building with the words "separation of church and state" still fresh on his mind.

Is this the practice of a leader committed to shuttering religion away from public life? Is this reflective of a fear that Christians might have too much influence in public affairs? Or is it evidence of a man who, while cautioning against a mandatory national belief system, strongly embraced the vitality of his own personal practice of devotion to God—even in public places?

Remember, the letter to the Connecticut Baptists had been written only two days before Jefferson found himself in the Capitol building listening to a sermon by Massachusetts Baptist minister John Leland. The Library of Congress exhibit asserts, "It is no exaggeration to say that on Sundays in Washington, during the administrations of Thomas Jefferson (1801-1809) and James Madison (1809-1817), the state became the church." Further, "In attending church services on public property," these Founders were "consciously and deliberately" making a statement about the priority of religion in public life.

So how have we come so far from the intent of these men? Recent forensic tests on the original Danbury letter (conducted for the Library of Congress by the Federal Bureau of Investigation Laboratory) reveal that Thomas Jefferson was intentional in not building an artificial barrier, purposefully weighing his words and revising his letter so that the influence of religion would be protected.

Have we believed a lie propagated by the modern U.S. Supreme Court? How ironic, especially since the Library of Congress specifically notes that during the Jefferson presidency, "The Gospel was also preached in the Supreme Court chambers." Yet today, the Supreme Court threatens the very fabric of freedom on which our nation was founded.

Their decisions have ramifications that extend far beyond the Supreme Court building. In fact, the result has been the censoring of religious expression from all aspects of public life. For example, in the spring of 2001, Attorney General John Ashcroft came under fire from the anti-faith media for holding Bible studies in his office at the Justice Department, even though the studies are totally voluntary. Instead of commending the Attorney General for honoring God at the start of each day, the ACLU and others attempted to bully Ashcroft into silence. Of course, they used their mistaken understanding of "separation of church and state" as the

D. James Kennedy

key piece of evidence in their case.

In the pages that follow, you will be challenged to become part of reclaiming the Founder's legacy of religious liberty. That legacy is described in great detail, historical event by historical event, in theory and in practice, in Archie Jones' excellent overview, "Church and State: The Federal Record." It is courageously championed by Alabama Chief Justice Roy Moore in his message, "God & Government: Ask the Founders," originally delivered to the 2001 Reclaiming America For Christ conference.

But it's not enough to simply be an astute student of history. It's not enough to just know the facts. We must act in response. We must act for the truth, for truth is on our side. In this book you will find significant action steps which you—as an American concerned for the intent of our Founders and concerned for the future of our nation—can take to help reverse the dangerous decline in our religious freedoms.

This is no easy task. The ACLU has been working for decades to purge our society of our cherished religious liberties. But as concerned citizens become educated and get involved, we will see our lost legacy of liberty restored. I hope and pray that this book will help toward that end.

D. James Kennedy

THE FIRST AMENDMENT: A LOST LEGACY

D. James Kennedy, Ph.D.

THE FIRST AMENDMENT:
A LOST LEGACY

D. James Kennedy, Ph.D.

In Pennsylvania a gentleman is arrested for the orderly preaching of the Gospel on a public street corner.

In Massachusetts certain bricks purchased by private citizens and inscribed with messages for a public park fundraiser are removed because they contain "religious" messages. All other messages remain by order of the city.

In New Jersey a class valedictorian is told to remove thanks to Jesus Christ from her valedictory address.

In Wisconsin an individual is prohibited from using a public library meeting room for a seminar on creation science.

In numerous cities and states around the country National Day of Prayer organizers are denied access to public meeting places.

What do these stories of government restrictions on religious liberty and speech have in common? Unfortunately, they share an erroneous interpretation of the First Amendment to the United States Constitution and a palpable hostility to the exercise of religious liberty and speech in the public arena.

In short, the last century has seen a growing hostility against religion in American public life and a corresponding use of the establishment clause of the First Amendment to "cleanse" the public square of any Christian content.

In each of the instances mentioned above, and countless others, a governmental entity used the so-called doctrine of the separation of church and state to deny public access to Christians and their views. In reality, the "separation of church and state," as it is popularly used, was unknown to the Founders of our country and played no significant part in our laws until the last half century.

The commonly held view of what the relationship between church and state should be is almost diametrically opposed to what was taught by the Founding Fathers. If unchecked, this trend of misinterpretation will bring about the beginning of the end of our religious liberties. Yet how many people understand what the First Amendment truly says?

Does the First Amendment teach the "separation of church and state"? Probably 99 percent of the people in America today have been brainwashed into saying "yes." But it does not!

We must understand what the First Amendment says, because the relationship between these two "kingdoms"—church and state—has been long and difficult. The Founding Fathers resolved that question in a marvelous way, but their solution is being completely disregarded in our time—and most people are not even aware of it.

The First Amendment actually states: "Congress shall make no law respecting an establishment of religion or prohibiting the free exercise thereof." What does this say about what the Church can or cannot do? What does it say about what a Christian citizen should or should not do? Absolutely nothing! It says, "Congress shall make no law respecting an establishment of religion or prohibiting the free exercise thereof."

The First Amendment forbids the federal government from restricting the free exercise of religion and the formation of a national church. Thus it was intended to keep the federal government from compelling worship and belief through a national church and to assure that Americans would always be free to exercise their faith as their consciences dictated.

Where, then, did we get this idea of a "wall of separation between church and state"? It comes not from the First Amendment, but from a private letter written in 1802 by Thomas Jefferson (who was not a member of the Constitutional Convention) to the Danbury Baptists in Connecticut. He stated his opinion that there should be "a wall of separation between church and state." Now, what is the difference between that so-called "wall of separation" and the actual wording of the First Amendment?

Our religious liberties depend on a proper perception of the difference between these two things. The First Amendment is a one-way street. It restrains the federal government. After the main body of the Constitution was completed, the Bill of Rights was written to keep the federal government from interfering with the liberties of the people. The Framers agreed to include the Bill of Rights (the first 10 amendments to

the Constitution) because they feared the people would not accept the new Constitution unless the rights of the people were more clearly defined and stated.

"A wall of separation," on the other hand, is most emphatically a two-way street. It prohibits and restrains those on one side of the wall as much as those on the other side. Instead of the one-way street the Framers originally intended for the First Amendment, Jefferson's opinion gradually gained preeminence so that, in practice, the amendment became a two-way street.

But in the last several decades, the First Amendment has been turned around again, until now we have virtually a one-way street … moving in the opposite direction. The phrase "separation of church and state" has come to mean what religion and, specifically, what the Christian Church shall or shall not do—180 degrees from the First Amendment!

The Supreme Court has been unshackling the federal government from the First Amendment and is placing these shackles on religion. Our freedoms are in jeopardy today, but most of us do not speak out against this danger because it has yet to affect us personally

As Roman Catholic scholar Rev. Joseph F. Costanzo wrote in his book, *This Nation Under God: Church, State and School in America*:

> There has been a full and truly vicious circle, from religious persecution, intolerance and church establishment to benign tolerance; to disestablishment; to equality of all faiths before the law; to equality of belief and non-belief before the law; and now to the secularists' and religious dissenters' intolerance of religious belief in public law. The wry irony is that this is being done in the name of religious liberty.[1]

Intolerance that was once shown by state religions toward those of other beliefs is now enacted publicly and legally by those holding a secular view of life against those who believe in God.

First Amendment History

To understand the current danger to our religious freedom, let us examine the development of the First Amendment: what its Framers originally intended it to mean, how the Supreme Court has altered this meaning in various rulings, and how the modern Court interprets it today. Once we clearly see this historical progression, it will be evident how radically the relationship between church and state has changed in the past 50 years.

When the First Amendment was adopted in 1791, its meaning and purpose were clear. The Articles of Confederation, our nation's first form of government after the Revolution, had failed to provide an effective central government. So, in 1787 our Constitution was drafted to replace the Articles, providing a stronger, yet still limited, federal government.

There was deep concern, however, that with its expanded powers, the federal government might be tempted to seize the rights of the states and the people, rights they had won in the still-recent Revolutionary War. Before the states ratified the Constitution, Congress promised to add the Bill of Rights to safeguard these freedoms and ensure the Constitution's passage.

The first words of the First Amendment deny Congress the power of making any laws establishing any particular religion or restricting the free exercise of any religion. Our Founders did not want the new government to have power over the religious lives and consciences of its citizens.

This amendment forbade the national government from establishing a national church and restricting in any manner the free practice of any religious faith. Since Congress alone was granted the authority to pass laws, it was not necessary to limit the power of the president or the courts. They were supposed to have been completely incapable of establishing a religion or restricting anyone from practicing his or her faith.

This amendment forbade the national government from establishing a national church and restricting in any manner the free practice of any religious faith.

This First Amendment prohibition applied only to the federal government and did not involve the state governments. Connecticut, Maryland, Massachusetts, New Hampshire and South Carolina each had established churches at the time the amendment was adopted. The federal government was forbidden to interfere with such state laws, and it could not attempt to overpower state religious convictions by establishing a federal church.

The federal government, as envisioned by our Founders, would be powerless to pass laws telling the states or the people how to (or how not to) practice their religious faith. This was the original meaning of the First Amendment.

After the Civil War, the 13th (1865), 14th (1868) and 15th (1870) Amendments were passed. They legally ended slavery, required that all citizens within a state be treated on an equal basis, and granted the right to vote to all male citizens. The 14th Amendment would become vitally important in discussions of the First Amendment. It reads:

> No state shall make or enforce any law which shall abridge the privileges or immunities of citizens of the United States; nor shall any state deprive any person of life, liberty, or property, without due process of law; nor deny to any person within its jurisdiction the equal protection of the laws.

Although the Supreme Court would eventually use this amendment to extend the First Amendment Establishment of Religion clause to the state governments, it was not understood this way at the time. President Ulysses Grant, a strong supporter of the absolute separation of church and state doctrine, wanted to force states to obey the same First Amendment restrictions already on the federal government. Yet, instead of employing the 14th Amendment, his supporters tried to do this through Congress.

In 1876, near the end of Grant's administration, the Blaine Amendment was introduced into Congress. Not only would this amendment have made the states unable to establish or restrict the free exercise of religion, it also would have stopped all government aid to parochial schools. But in 1876, the amendment failed to garner the necessary votes in the Senate and was defeated. Although it would be reintroduced in Congress year after year, the Blaine Amendment never received enough support to pass. Years later, however, the Supreme Court made the Blaine Amendment unnecessary by changing the original meaning of the First Amendment through its own arbitrary decree.

Hard Cases

Until 1925, the Court had ruled that the 14th Amendment had not made the Bill of Rights applicable to the states, except where this was "implicit in the concept of ordered liberty." The First Amendment was still seen as a restriction on the power of Congress, not the states.

Slowly, however, in a series of decisions in hard cases between 1925 and 1931, the Court began to claim the authority to bind state

Slowly ... the Court begant to claim the authority to bind state governments by the Bill of Rights rather than their own state constitutions. The growth in judicial power was small, but it would later mushroom.

governments by the Bill of Rights rather than their own state constitutions. The growth in judicial power was small, but it would later mushroom.

The fateful day was May 29, 1940, more than seven decades after the 14th Amendment and 150 years after the adoption of the Constitution. In all that time, the First Amendment had never applied to the states. Yet, on this day the Court decided otherwise in *Cantwell v. Connecticut*.

Newton Cantwell and his two sons were Jehovah's Witnesses. At that time, the message of the Jehovah's Witnesses was very derogatory toward the Roman Catholic faith, claiming it was a fraud—a religious racket. The Cantwells publicly presented this message (using a phonograph record) to two Catholic men, who called the police. The Cantwells were charged with not having a license to solicit funds and with inciting a breach of the peace, even though these charges did not properly apply. The Cantwells were convicted, and the case was eventually appealed to the Supreme Court.

It was clear to the Court that an injustice had occurred, but the proposed remedy went far beyond the facts in the case. It was here that the Court first proclaimed this sweeping judgment:

> The First Amendment declares that Congress shall make no law respecting an establishment of religion or prohibiting the free exercise thereof. The Fourteenth Amendment has rendered the legislatures of the states as incompetent as Congress to enact such laws.

Since establishment of religion was not an issue in this case, the ruling made only the free exercise clause applicable to the states. The Cantwells' conviction was reversed, but unfortunately the power of the Supreme Court over the states was greatly increased.

In a number of cases concerning the rights of the Jehovah's Witnesses (to not salute the flag in school, to assemble, and to distribute literature), the Court, concerned about the social value of patriotism, ruled against them. But by 1942 the Court reversed itself, providing the Witnesses with legal protection from official persecution and discrimination.

Although the conscience rights of the Witnesses needed protection, these cases made clear that the states would now be required to enforce the First Amendment. While this had advantages, it now became the task of the Supreme Court to determine the states' compliance with the Constitution.

The far-flung extent to which the Supreme Court was now involved in the question of religion and government appeared in two further cases.

In the first case, *United States v. Ballard* (1944), George W. Ballard had begun a faith-healing religious movement called "I Am." After his death, Ballard's wife and son continued the movement, which was very profitable. In time, they were charged with using the mails to defraud. The case normally would have demanded that they be shown to have made false statements in order to gain money and that they knew at the time the statements were false.

The district court felt uneasy about the case since it seemed to be judging the Ballards' religion, which hardly seemed proper. Therefore, the judge told the jury that the question was not whether the Ballards could heal, but whether they believed they could heal. Although the judge thought this instruction helped protect religious freedom, in fact, this only made the Ballards' conviction easier to obtain, since they had to produce evidence substantiating their belief in their ability to heal.

The Ballards were convicted, but the appellate court, which correctly reasoned that the burden of proof was the government's, reversed their conviction. Their conviction was eventually upheld by the Supreme Court, which agreed with the district court, holding that it was the role of the judicial branch to prosecute religious teachers based on the sincerity of their faith. Justice Robert H. Jackson disagreed with the majority's ruling. He said:

> The price of freedom of religion or of speech or of the
> press is that we must put up with, and even pay for, a
> good deal of rubbish.... I would dismiss the indictment
> and have done with this business of judicially examining
> other people's faith.[2]

In the name of protecting religious liberty, the Court actually lowered the requirement of proof necessary to find the Ballards guilty and, in fact, limited their religious freedom. (This does not mean that the Ballards were sincere, but only that it is not the federal courts' role to make such rulings.) This case greatly increased the power of the courts.

The second case, *Girouard v. United States* (1946), had to deal with a prospective citizen who, because of his Seventh-Day Adventist faith, was opposed to all warfare. In 1929 the Supreme Court ruled that any person who refused to take a legally required oath indicating a willingness to take up arms to defend the country could not be naturalized. The issue had been controversial, and attempts had been made in Congress to change the oath. In the Naturalization Act of 1940, however, the oath remained unchanged.

When the *Girouard* case came before the Supreme Court, the justices ruled that the oath was unconstitutional, citing Article VI of the Constitution, which forbade the federal government from requiring a religious test for office—despite the fact that it was a person's citizenship at stake, not an office of any kind. They said, in effect, that this oath was an unconstitutional religious test because it went against the beliefs of religious pacifists.

In this action the Court effectively amended the Naturalization Act in a manner that Congress had been unable to do in 11 years of debate. The justices were now writing laws concerning the proper relationship between the federal government and religion. It is clear that the writers of the Constitution never intended for Article VI to apply to the naturalization of citizens. The Court was now finding "rights" that were not objectively stated.

The next change in the understanding of the First Amendment came in 1947. In *Everson v. Board of Education* the issue was public funds used to help pay for the transportation of students, regardless of whether they went to public or private schools. Some of these schools were parochial. Arch R. Everson claimed this was inappropriate government support of religion.

Although the Court ruled against *Everson*, it radically changed the historical understanding of the Establishment clause. Justice Hugo Black stated in this decision:

The "establishment of religion" clause of the First Amendment means at least this: Neither a state nor the Federal

Justice Hugo Black. Photograph by Harris and Ewing, collection of the Supreme Court of the United States.

Government can set up a church. Neither can pass laws which aid one religion, aid all religions, or prefer one religion over another.[3]

Simply by adding the three words, "aid all religions," Justice Black added a new, revolutionary concept to the First Amendment.

Simply by adding the three words, "aid all religions," Justice Black added a new, revolutionary concept to the First Amendment. These three words would become the basis the Court would use to attack the financial foundation of religious education in America and remove all mention of God from the public schools.

Justice Black also declared in this decision that "The First Amendment has erected a wall between church and state. That wall must be kept high and impregnable. We could not approve the slightest breach." Thus Jefferson's concept of the "wall of separation between church and state" was introduced into the interpretation of the First Amendment.

By interpreting the Establishment clause this way, the free exercise of religion was limited by government power only to the non-public sphere. The Supreme Court could now issue rulings governing what was a permissible expression of religious faith, if in any manner it was related to public land, government or funds. Lecturer and author George Goldberg, a graduate of Harvard Law School, has called this ruling "the federal takeover of religion in America."[4]

Justice Black's interpretation of the Establishment clause ignored the historical reality that the government had been aiding religion in a non-discriminatory manner from this nation's inception. His interpretation was at variance with the tradition, law and practice of our nation.

The new revolutionary viewpoint of Justice Black would become clear when the issue of released time came before the Court in *McCollum v. Board of Education* (1948). Some public schools in the 1940s allowed students to be voluntarily released with the permission of their parents for a half-hour of religious instruction a week in the faith of their preference. Such programs had been conducted since before World War I. These classes, conducted by clergymen on school property, were popular with the children and well-attended in most cases.

When one child in Champaign, Illinois, did not attend these classes, school officials put undue pressure on the child and his parents to have him attend. His mother sued in 1944 and in 1948 won her case before the Supreme Court.

The one dissenting vote in *McCollum*, Justice Stanley F. Reed, pointed out that Thomas Jefferson, who had written about a "wall of separation," did not restrict pupils from receiving religious instruction at the University of Virginia. He stated:

Thus the "wall of separation between church and state" that Mr. Jefferson built at the University which he founded did not exclude religious education from the school. The difference between the generality of his statements on the separation of church and state and the specificity of his conclusions on education are considerable. *A rule of law should not be drawn from a figure of speech* (emphasis added).[5]

In his opinion for the majority, Justice Black essentially relied on only four historical documents: Madison's "Remonstrance" and "Detached Memoranda" and Jefferson's "Bill for Religious Liberty" and the "Danbury Baptist" letter. In so doing, he ignored the many other writings and actions of Jefferson, Madison, the Congress and other presidents, which clearly indicated that the First Amendment rejected a national church and the preference of one sect over another and did not deny aid to religion when this was done in a non-discriminatory manner. Justice Black went further than Thomas Jefferson would have ever imagined in the attempt to separate religion from the state.

The Supreme Court, rather than strictly judging whether the program in Champaign had been conducted correctly (and if, in fact, the program was using official coercion to have students attend religious classes), banned all such programs throughout the nation as unconstitutional—regardless of how they were conducted.

This meant that not only must a child be allowed to abstain, but that all students must be forced to abstain, so that none would feel compelled to attend. Government could not be seen as aiding religion even when this was non-discriminatory and participation was voluntary. The rights of thousands of students to exercise their faith were restricted to avoid the possibility of even one student being coerced into involvement in a religious exercise.

McCollum brought a great deal of confusion. School administrators, teachers, and parents throughout the country wondered what the law of the land allowed. Were all religious instruction and expression in school now illegal? What of school prayer, Bible reading, Christmas plays, the singing of Handel's Messiah—or even "God Bless America"? If it was wrong for government to "aid all religions" in any way, where did one draw the line?

Reign of Confusion

This confusion spilled over to the Court. Now that the justices had to sit in judgment on what was permissible religious practice, a lack of consistency began to show up in their rulings. In a series of cases, the Court attempted to set forth what it felt was the proper balance between the Free Exercise and Establishment clauses.

First, the Court decided in *Saia v. New York* (1948) that state and city governments could not ban the use of loudspeakers to preach to others on public property, even when there were complaints of disturbing the peace and harassment. Then, the Court held in *Kunz v. People of the State of New York* (1951) that a man in the midst of a Jewish community could proclaim a message of hate toward all Jews and a wish that they had all been killed in the Holocaust, since this was part of his religious faith and not merely "fighting words" (which have never been protected under freedom of speech). In *Zorach v. Clauson* (1952), the Court decided that a New York released time program was constitutional since its classes were not held on school property but, instead, were conducted in church buildings.

The justices also supported Sunday blue laws in several 1961 rulings (*McGowan v. State of Maryland, Braunfeld v. Brown, Gallagher v. Crown Kosher Super Market*). They did so even though it was demonstrated that this created a financial hardship and constituted unfair competition for Jews and others who held to a Saturday Sabbath. Goldberg remarked at the confused religious double standard employed by the Court:

> [T]he Court, which had upheld the right of a Witness to shatter the peace on a Sunday with a public address system, and of a hatemonger to call every day from a well-traveled street corner for the extermination of the Jews, held that, where state law requires it, Jews must observe the Christian Sabbath.[6]

In *Engel v. Vitale* (1962) the Supreme Court, by a 6-1 margin, reversed two lower courts and declared unconstitutional a strictly voluntary, non-denominational school prayer composed by the New York Board of Regents. Before the case went to the Supreme Court, the chief justice of the New York Court of Appeals stated in his opinion that:

> Not only is this prayer not a violation of the First Amendment ... but a holding that it is such a violation would be in defiance of all American history, and such a holding would destroy a part of the essential foundation of the American governmental structures.[7]

When the Supreme Court held that it was a violation, the country was shocked. The Court was now stating that a practice that had been part of American life since the colonization of the continent was unconstitutional. While some believed the ban only proscribed state-composed prayers, many leading legal scholars felt sure that this decision would eliminate from the public schools Bible reading, prayer recitation, the celebration of religious holidays, and all religious practices.

Not quite a year later, on June 17, 1963, the Supreme Court did what many people feared. In a Baltimore suit, *Murray v. Curlett*, instituted by avowed atheist Madelyn Murray (later O'Hair), and in a Pennsylvania case, *School District of Abington Township v. Schempp*, the justices ruled it was unconstitutional for a state to have portions of the Bible recited in schools. Despite the fact that any student who wished was excused, the Court labeled this an establishment of religion. In his concurring opinion to the 8-1 decision, Justice William Brennan said the fact that the state had not composed the religious material was "constitutionally irrelevant."

Justice Potter Stewart, the lone dissenting vote, blasted the ruling, saying it led not to true neutrality with respect to religion, but to the "establishment of a religion of secularism."[8]

This decision made clear that it was prayer that was banned, not simply state-written prayers. On June 19, 1963, *The Wall Street Journal* commented that atheism was now "the one belief to which the state's power will extend its protection." In light of this case, some states banned all prayers and Bible reading. A lower court even decreed that kindergarten children could not pray "God is great, God is good, and we thank Him for our food. Amen" (*Stein v. Oshinsky*). That such

Justice Potter Stewart, the lone dissenting vote, blasted the ruling, saying it led not to true neutrality with respect to religion, but to the "establishment of a religion of secularism."

things would become prohibited by force of law in a free society is almost beyond belief.

The Supreme Court then stepped back from its attempt to build an impregnable wall between religion and the public domain. In *Walz v. Tax Commission of the City of New York* (1970), the Court said that the tax-exempt status of religious institutions was constitutional. The reasoning of new Chief Justice Warren Burger is explained by two experts on constitutional history, Dr. Alfred Kelly and Dr. Winfred Harrison:

> ... the Court by an eight to one vote accepted the constitutionality of a New York law exempting church-owned real property from taxation. Similar exemptions, the Chief Justice pointed out, were obtained in all fifty states; moreover, the practice was at least two hundred years old and was "deeply embedded in our national life." Tax exemption, Burger continued, could not properly be equated with direct monetary grants to churches. On the contrary, he thought, it probably did more to preserve "a benevolent neutrality" toward organized religion than would church taxation, what with its potential element of entanglement.[9]

It was clear that the Supreme Court was aware of the dangers of its earlier decisions and how, if taken to an extreme, they could have a devastating effect on every religious organization within the United States. However, even greater confusion lay ahead.

Just ten months after *Walz*, the Court in *Lemon v. Kurtzman* (1971), ruled unconstitutional Rhode Island and Pennsylvania's salary supplements and subsidies to instructors in private schools teaching secular subjects. Chief Justice Burger set forth a confusing three-part test to determine what was an establishment of religion. This test states:

It was clear that the Supreme Court was aware of the dangers of its earlier decisions and how, if taken to an extreme, they could have a devastating effect on every religious organization within the United States.

> First, the statute must have a secular legislative purpose; second, its principal or primary effect must be one that

neither advances nor inhibits religion; finally, the statute must not foster an excessive government entanglement with religion.[10]

Although Chief Justice Burger did not know it at the time, his three-part test would force the Court to strain at gnats and swallow camels.

Although Chief Justice Burger did not know it at the time, his three-part test would force the Court to strain at gnats and swallow camels.

On the same day the Chief Justice set forth this test, the Court did not find unconstitutional direct federal aid to building projects on religious institutions (*Tilton v. Richardson*), a much more extensive program than the Rhode Island and Pennsylvania supplements to private school teachers struck down in Lemon.

It was becoming clear that with the willingness to forget the historical meaning of the First Amendment, it could mean whatever a majority of the justices felt like making it mean. This attitude is well summed up by former U.S. Representative John B. Conlan, from Arizona:

> The Constitution is no better than the five out of nine men that you have on the Supreme Court at any point in time. What the constitutional fathers meant when they created that document and that contract among the people is one thing. It may not mean the same to someone else two hundred years later, even though it should. But depending on whom you have in the presidency and whom you have in the Senate, who confirms or rejects presidential appointments, will determine what your Constitution means, if anything at all. The fact that we have a great Constitution, in itself, means nothing.[11]

Now such a situation cannot give people any solid protection of their "unalienable rights" or security that the basic legal structure of society is stable. Rather the citizen, institution and state are cast into a relativistic sea in which massive changes in the law can take place very rapidly without due process. Without a Constitution followed by the rules of historical interpretation—in an attempt to reflect the intent of the authors of the law—we are left to the subjective whims of the majority of the Court.

The 1970s: Arbitrary Judicial Power

In 1972, the justices exempted Amish children (but not Jewish or Catholic children) from a state-required school curriculum at age 14 instead of 16, the state-mandated age (*Wisconsin v. Yoder*). (However, in 1982, in *U.S. v. Lee*, they would force them to pay social security tax for their employees, even though this was in direct violation of their religious convictions.) Also in 1972, the Court decided that the armed services could not require students at their academies to attend worship services (*Anderson v. Laird*). But unlike the reasoning it used in *McCollum*, the Court did not rule that the mere existence of these services on public property was unconstitutional.

The Court, in 1973, declared unconstitutional an attempt by New York state to reimburse low-income parents a portion of tuition costs to provide their children with private education (*Committee for Public Education and Religious Liberty v. Nyquist*). It also prohibited the state from reimbursing private schools for giving state-required examinations to students (*Levitt v. Committee for Public Education and Religious Liberty*).

In *Meek v. Pettinger* (1975), Pennsylvania's law providing "secular, neutral, non-ideological" books, instructional materials, and equipment to private and religious schools (the same as were provided for public school children) was ruled unconstitutional, despite the fact that Pennsylvania had attempted to write its statute in light of the *Lemon* test. It also should be mentioned that Chief Justice Burger himself felt his test was being applied in an inflexible and doctrinaire manner.

Justice William Rehnquist commented in dissent to *Meek*:

> I am disturbed as much by the overtones of the Court's opinion as by its actual holding. The Court apparently believes that the Establishment Clause of the First Amendment not only mandates religious neutrality on the part of the government, but also requires that this Court go further and throw its weight on the side of those who believe that our society as a whole should be a purely secular one. Nothing in the First Amendment or in the cases interpreting it requires such an extreme approach.[12]

The arbitrary nature of the Court's ruling was clear. A Maryland law providing government support to private colleges, almost identical to the law struck down in Pennsylvania in *Meek*, was declared by a 5-4 vote to be constitutional in 1976 (*Roemer v. Board of Public Works of*

Maryland). The Court was so divided on the issue that five separate opinions were rendered.

In 1977, the Supreme Court found itself deciding extremely minor matters on constitutional grounds. In *Wooley v. Maynard* the majority of the justices determined that a message ("Live Free or Die") placed on license plates by New Hampshire was an infringement of the rights of a Jehovah's Witness who disagreed with the message.

In 1978, in *McDaniel v. Paty*, the Court ruled that no state constitution could have a greater degree of separation between religion and state than that set forth by the First Amendment, as interpreted by the Supreme Court. Therefore, a state constitution forbidding clergymen from serving as legislators was declared unconstitutional. The federal standard and only the federal standard was to be the law of the land.

The 1980s: Judicial Micromanagement

Many observers anticipated that the 1980s would bring a significant change to the United States Supreme Court. With conservative presidents Reagan and Bush in the White House, it was expected that conservative jurists would replace retiring liberal justices. Conservative court watchers hailed the appointments of Sandra Day O'Connor, Antonin Scalia, Anthony Kennedy, David Souter and Clarence Thomas, and the elevation of William Rehnquist to Chief Justice.

With conservative presidents Reagan and Bush in the White House, it was expected that conservative jurists would replace retiring liberal justices.

While these justices exerted significant influence over the direction of the Court, no "Reagan Revolution" took place in America's judiciary. While some gains were made, other losses offset these modest victories.

Ideological differences between the justices became more pronounced through the decade. Deep divisions between liberals and conservatives gave rise to a series of narrowly decided rulings. As a result of strong differences over how (or if) the *Lemon* test should be applied, the Supreme Court began to micromanage the relationship between church and state. Hairsplitting decisions were made on the basis of very specific facts rather than general principles of liberty.

For example, the Supreme Court in 1980 upheld by a 5-4 vote a New York law regarding the reimbursement of private and religious institutions for administering state-required tests (*Committee for Public*

Education v. Regan). The law upheld was nearly identical to the one struck down in *Nyquist* seven years earlier. In 1983, again by a 5-4 vote, the Court upheld state tax deductions for parents sending their children to parochial schools (*Mueller v. Allen*). But in 1985, in *Grand Rapids v. Ball* and in *Aguilar v. Felton*, the Supreme Court struck down other forms of aid to parochial education.

In 1985, the Supreme Court struck down a state law granting employees an absolute right to abstain from work on the Sabbath (*Thornton v. Caldor*). On the other hand, in 1987, the Court ruled that a worker was entitled to unemployment compensation after being discharged for refusing to work on her Sabbath (*Hobbie v. Unemployment Appeals Commission of Florida*).

Lack of consistency brought about by the *Lemon* test is further evidenced by the Supreme Court's treatment of public Christmas displays. In 1984, the Court ruled that the city of Pawtucket, Rhode Island, did not violate the Establishment Clause by including a crèche scene in the city's annual holiday display.[13] On the other hand, in the 1989 case, *Allegheny County v. ACLU*, a plurality decision from a deeply divided Court struck down a nativity scene inside a county courthouse, while upholding a Menorah and Christmas tree on the steps of another government building.

The Court further compounded the confusion by ruling two ways on the question of the privacy of religious institutions. In *Amos v. Corporation of the Presiding Bishop of the Church of Jesus Christ of Latter Day Saints*, the Court held that churches may practice job discrimination based on creed and ethical conduct, even when the job in question is nonreligious in nature. On the other hand, in *Bob Jones University v. United States*, the Court decided that the government could revoke a religious university's tax-exempt status based on that university's religiously motivated refusal to allow dating between people of different races. While we understand the Court's concern with racial prejudice, it must be understood that the school's policy was based on sincerely held religious convictions. Essentially, the Court ruled that the government is free to tax unpopular religious beliefs on the basis of what the justices conceive to be better public policy.[14]

On public prayer, the Court ruled in *Marsh v. Chambers* (1983) that a Presbyterian minister could be paid by the state of Nebraska to be the chaplain of the state legislature and could even have his prayers printed at public expense. Chief Justice Burger himself ruled:

In light of the unambiguous and unbroken history of more than 200 years, there can be no doubt that the practice of opening legislative sessions with prayer has become part of the fabric of our society. To invoke Divine guidance on a public body entrusted with making the laws is not, in these circumstances, an establishment of religion or a step toward establishment; it is simply a tolerable acknowledgment of beliefs widely held among the people of this country.[15]

Of course, what the Chief Justice wrote was true. But although the same could be said of prayer and Bible reading in schools, the Court did not act upon this logic. In fact, the Supreme Court dealt harshly with state laws regarding religion in the public schools. In 1985, the Supreme Court struck down an Alabama law authorizing a "moment of silence" in public schools for the purpose of prayer (*Wallace v. Jaffree*).

In one of the most compelling dissents ever written by a Supreme Court Justice, William Rehnquist decried the seemingly contradictory results yielded by the *Lemon* test:

Chief Justice William H. Rehnquist (1972-). Collection, The Supreme Court Historical Society. Photograph by Dane Penland, Smithsonian Institution.

These difficulties arise because the *Lemon* test has no more grounding in the history of the First Amendment than does the wall theory upon which it rests.... The three-part test has simply not provided adequate standards for deciding Establishment Clause cases, as this Court has slowly come to realize. Even worse, the *Lemon* test has caused this Court to fracture into unworkable plurality opinions... depending upon how each of the three factors applies to a certain state action. The results from our school services cases show the difficulty we have encountered in making the *Lemon* test yield principled results.

For example, a state may lend to parochial schoolchildren geography textbooks that contain maps of the United

States, but the state may not lend maps of the United States for use in geography class. A state may lend textbooks on American colonial history, but it may not lend a film on George Washington, or a film projector to show it in history class. A state may lend classroom workbooks, but may not lend workbooks in which the parochial schoolchildren write, thus rendering them non-reusable. A state may pay for bus transportation to religious schools, but may not pay for bus transportation from the parochial school to the public zoo or natural history museum for a field trip. A state may pay for diagnostic services conducted in the parochial school, but therapeutic services must be given in a different building; speech and hearing "services" conducted by the state inside the sectarian school are forbidden … but the state may conduct speech and hearing diagnostic testing inside the sectarian school. Exceptional parochial school students may receive counseling, but it must take place outside of the parochial school, such as in a trailer parked down the street. A state may give cash to a parochial school to pay for the administration of state-written tests and state-ordered reporting services, but it may not provide funds for teacher-prepared tests on secular subjects. Religious instruction may not be given in public school, but the public school may release students during the day for religion classes elsewhere, and may enforce attendance at those classes with its truancy laws. …

It is not surprising in the light of this record that our most recent opinions have expressed doubt on the usefulness of the *Lemon* test.[16]

Nevertheless, the *Lemon* test continued to be employed throughout the 1980s. State laws dealing with religion in the public schools were particularly targeted by the High Court. In *Stone v. Graham*, the justices voted 5-4 to overturn a Kentucky law requiring the Ten Commandments to be posted in public schools. In 1987, a Louisiana law requiring public schools to afford balanced treatment to evolution and creation science was struck down in *Edwards v. Aguillard*.

The 1990s-Present: High Hopes Deferred

The alarming trend to isolate public school students from all religious influences was dealt a temporary blow in the early 1990s. In the 1990 case, *Westside Community Schools v. Mergens*, the Supreme Court ruled 8-1 that students have a right to form voluntary Bible Clubs on public high school campuses in some circumstances. Specifically, the justices upheld a 1984 federal law, the Equal Access Act, that required school administrators to treat all non-curriculum student clubs equally, regardless of political, philosophical or religious content.[17] Writing for the majority, Justice Sandra Day O'Connor stated:

> There is a crucial difference between government speech endorsing religion, which the Establishment Clause forbids, and private speech endorsing religion, which the Free Speech and Free Exercise clauses protect.

A means of religious expression was kept open to high school students to reach out to their peers with the Gospel of Christ. Just as significantly, the justices expressly ruled the Constitution's guarantee of free speech protected religious ideas expressed in public settings.

But that same year the Supreme Court dramatically changed its view of the Free Exercise Clause. In *Employment Division v. Smith*, the Supreme Court ruled that the First Amendment does not require states to create religious exemptions to generally applicable laws that burden the free exercise of religion. Specifically, the Court majority stated that Oregon was not constitutionally required to exempt the religious use of peyote, a hallucinogen used in Native American rituals, from its regulations governing the conduct of the state's drug rehabilitation counselors.

A means of religious expression was kept open to high school students to reach out to their peers with the Gospel of Christ. Just as significantly, the justices expressly ruled the Constitution's guarantee of free speech protected religious ideas expressed in public settings.

Justice Scalia, writing for the majority, largely abandoned the "compelling state interest test" first articulated by liberal Justice William Brennan in 1962. This test required the government to demonstrate that it had a compelling obligation whenever it passed a law that impacted an activity that was central to a person's religious faith. The religious needs of the individual were balanced against the "compelling interest" of the government. In this judicial balancing act, the government generally won.

Critics lambasted Justice Scalia for abandoning this legal test. Although not a very good test, at least it was *something* to prevent government's wanton interference in religious practices. Others, however, recognized that Scalia's ruling abandoned a test that was invented in the 1960s by a liberal justice in favor of a more historical approach. In this view, *Smith* is closer to the federalist ideals of the Founding Fathers. As discussed earlier, the First Amendment did not originally apply to the states, but only limited Congress. In *Smith*, the Supreme Court announced its intention to step back from strict oversight of state governments and the micromanagement of relations between church and state.

> *Critics lambasted Justice Scalia for abandoning this legal test. Although not a very good test, at least it was something to prevent government's wanton interference in religious practices.*

Speculation that the Supreme Court would also rethink its earlier reasoning regarding the Establishment Clause and abandon the flawed *Lemon* test ran rampant during deliberations in *Lee v. Weisman*. This case challenged traditional invocations and benedictions at high school graduation exercises. The Bush Administration, through the Department of Justice, submitted arguments calling upon the Supreme Court justices to abandon the *Lemon* test in favor of a more historical approach.

They did not. On June 24, 1992, a deeply divided Supreme Court ruled 5-4 against public schools in Providence, Rhode Island. The Court majority held that the direct involvement of schools in the construction of the prayers (by requiring clergy to pray according to certain guidelines) unconstitutionally entangled government with religion. Further, the Court ruled that school-sponsored graduation prayers forced individuals to support or participate in a religious exercise.

Justice Kennedy wrote the majority opinion in *Lee*. In doing so, he apparently contradicted what he had written just three years earlier in the 1989 nativity scene case, *Allegheny County v. ACLU*:

> A test for implementing the protections of the
> Establishment Clause that, if applied with consistency,
> would invalidate longstanding traditions cannot be a
> proper reading of the Clause. [18]

Nevertheless, the Supreme Court struck down a tradition of prayer in *Lee* that was as old as public school commencement exercises themselves. While prayer in schools continued to baffle the Supreme Court in the early 1990s, several positive decisions occurred that benefit people of religious faith. In the case of *Lukumi Babalu Ayue, Inc. v. City of Hialeah* (1993), the Court held that the government may not discriminate against an individual because of his or her religion. Unfortunately, the *Lukumi* decision occurred in the context of a religious sect's ritual sacrifice of animals. The Court held that a municipal ordinance that discriminated against the sect's practice of ritual sacrifice violated the Free Exercise Clause. The *Lukumi* decision has, however, been used to benefit Christians where a government entity has intentionally discriminated against the free exercise of religion.

While prayer in schools continued to baffle the Supreme Court in the early 1990s, several positive decisions occurred that benefit people of religious faith.

In *Zobrest v. Catalina Foothills School District* (1993), the Court ruled that providing certain special education service (an interpreter for a hearing impaired child) to a Catholic student was not prohibited by the Establishment Clause. Seven years later, in *Mitchell v. Helms*, the Court strengthened this view by holding that certain other specific forms of aid provided to Christian schools, such as library books or educational equipment, are constitutional.

In 1995, government-backed suppression of religious expression was dealt a significant blow in *Rosenberger v. Rector & Visitors*. The University of Virginia denied funding to pay for printing a student publication with a Christian perspective, while funding secular publications with different messages. The Supreme Court held that such a denial was viewpoint-based discrimination contrary to free speech rights. While the Court was sharply divided (a 5-4 majority), the result is that religious publications are entitled to government funds on equal terms with other private publications eligible for a state subsidy.

Unfortunately, the hope raised by several cases in the early to mid-1990s must be deferred. With the exception of Helms, positive Supreme Court decisions dealing with First Amendment religious liberties have been virtually non-existent. The Court continued its purging of the public school system of all religious influence in *Doe v. Santa Fe Independent School District* (2000). In *Doe*, the Court struck down a Texas school district's student free speech policy that allowed student-led, student-initiated messages—including prayers—at football games. Chief Justice Rehnquist, writing in dissent, noted that the Court's opinion "...bristles with hostility to all things religious in public life." As a new millennium dawned, the threat to religion in public life was as strong and dangerous as ever.

> *As a new millennium dawned, the threat to religion in public life was as strong and dangerous as ever.*

Notes

1. Rev. Joseph F. Costanzo, *This Nation Under God: Church, State and School in America* (1964), p. 131, quoted by George Goldberg, *Reconstructing America* (Grand Rapids: William B. Eerdmans Publishing Company, 1984), p. 122.
2. Goldberg, p. 38.
3. *Everson v. Board of Education*, 330 U.S. 1, at 15-16, quoted by Robert L. Cord, *Separation of Church and State*, (New York: Lambeth Press, 1982), p. 109.
4. Goldberg, p. 47.
5. Cord, p. 139.
6. Goldberg, p. 61.
7. Court of appeals decision is found at 10 N.Y. 2d 174, 218 N.Y. Supp.2d 659, 176 N.E.2d 579 (1961), quoted by Goldberg, p. 64.
8. Alfred H. Kelly and Winfred A. Harrison, *The American Constitution: Its Origin and Development* (New York: W. W. Norton and Company, 1976), p. 976.
9. Kelly and Harrison, p. 996.
10. *Lemon v. Kurtzman*, 403 U.S. 602 at 612, 613 (1971), quoted by Goldberg, p. 74.
11. Quoted in John W. Whitehead, *The Separation Illusion* (Milford, Mich: Mott Media, 1977), p. 124.
12. *Meek v. Pettinger*, 421 U.S. 349 at 395 (1975), quoted by Goldberg, p. 81-82.
13. Although the crèche scene was provided and illuminated at public expense, the overall display included enough secular symbols of the holiday that it passed the justice's scrutiny. Critics charged that the Supreme Court invented a "plastic reindeer rule" requiring all Christian symbols on public property to be diluted by sufficient numbers of pagan or secular symbols.
14. It should be noted that from a biblical perspective there is only one race—not many—descended from Adam. Although people have different skin colors and cultures, they are all made in God's image and are of the same race. The concept of different races is based on an evolutionary worldview rather than one based on creation.

15. *Marsh v. Chambers*, 103 S. Ct. 3330 (1983), quoted by Goldberg, p. 103.
16. *Wallace v. Jaffree*, 472 U.S. 38 (1985) (J. Rehnquist, dissenting).
17. Bridget Mergens and other students had been repeatedly denied permission to organize a campus Bible Club. In 1990 the U.S. Supreme Court ruled 8-1 that the school had discriminated against the students on the basis of their religious beliefs and had violated the 1984 Equal Access Act. The High Court upheld the Act and affirmed that student-initiated religious expression does not violate the Establishment Clause.
18. *Allegheny County v. ACLU*, 492 U.S. 573 at 670 (1989).

Section Two

CHURCH AND STATE: THE FEDERAL RECORD

Archie P. Jones, Ph.D.

CHURCH AND STATE: THE FEDERAL RECORD

Archie P. Jones, Ph.D.

*Congress shall make no law respecting an establishment
of religion, or prohibiting the free exercise thereof; or
abridging the freedom of speech, or of the press, or the
right of the people peaceably to assemble, and to petition
the Government for a redress of grievances.*

—The First Amendment to the U.S. Constitution

Neither the text of the First Amendment, nor its historical background,[1] nor the record of its formation[2] supports the notion that its framers and ratifiers intended to divorce "religion"—Christianity—from the conduct of our national government or the making of its laws. All the relevant factors support the idea that Christianity was intended to be influential in the making of our laws, the conduct of our civil government—even at the national level—and our public life.

In 1947 the United States Supreme Court read Thomas Jefferson's extra-constitutional 1802 phrase about "a wall of separation between church and state" into the Constitution and over previous U.S. Supreme Courts' interpretations of the "religion clauses" of the First Amendment. Since at least that time we have been beset by two prevalent misinterpretations, or false interpretations, of the intended meaning of the "religion clauses" of the First Amendment and of the intended role of "religion" in American civil government, law and public life.

The first of these false interpretations should be called "religious neutrality" or "religious neutralism." It is usually called "religious pluralism" or "nonpreferentialism." It holds that the intention of the religion clauses of the First Amendment was to make American civil government, law and public life "neutral" among all the religions of man, giving no preference to Christianity (or any other religion) over all the other religions of man.[3]

The second false interpretation should be called "secularism." It is usually called "absolute separationism," for it contends that the intention behind the religion clauses of the First Amendment was to establish a "wall of separation" between religion in general—and Christianity in particular—and American civil government, law and public life. The leading advocates of this notion contend that the intention behind the First Amendment was to forbid all federal or national government support of Christianity or any other religion, or for "religion" as such.[4]

Both of these false interpretations of the First Amendment agree that Christianity should not be permitted to exercise a dominant, formative influence on our national government and law. Their thrust is, in effect, to require a de-Christianization of American civil government, law and public life. For, as the evidence summarized below plainly indicates, Christianity was predominant in American civil government, law and public life not only before, but also during and long after the framing and ratification of the Constitution and the Bill of Rights.

Both religious neutrality and secularism are contrary to all the relevant facts concerning the framing and ratification of the Constitution, the Bill of Rights, and the First Amendment. Their arguments are contradicted by the facts of

- the predominantly Christian religious and ethical views of the American people for whom the Constitution was framed and ratified;[5]
- the plainly Christian nature of the education received by early Americans and their statesmen—before, during, and after the framing and ratification of the Constitution, Bill of Rights, and the First Amendment;[6]
- the clearly Christian nature of early American law, legal thought, and legal education before, during, and after the framing and ratification of the Constitution, the Bill of Rights, and the First Amendment;[7]
- the predominantly Christian nature of early American political thought;[8]
- the overwhelmingly Christian nature of the sources which were cited as authoritative by early American political writers and commentators from the period of independence through the era of constitution making;[9]
- the dominantly Christian nature of American leadership during and after the movement for independence;
- the Christian nature of our early states' constitutions, declarations

of rights, and bills of rights, before, during, and after the framing and ratification of the First Amendment;[10]
- the relationship between religion (Christianity), civil government, and law in the several states—before, during and long after the framing and ratification of the First Amendment;[11]
- the Christian religious faith of the overwhelming number and percentage of the men who framed and ratified our Constitution and Bill of Rights;[12]
- the Christian rhetoric of the Constitution;[13]
- the reasons for the Constitution's prohibition of a religious test for federal office;[14]
- the logic of the reasons why James Madison (with the support of others) proposed the addition of a Bill of Rights to the Constitution;[15] and
- the debates in the First Congress which produced what became the First Amendment and the Bill of Rights.[16]

Religious neutralist and secularist arguments simply cannot withstand an investigation of the relevant evidence.

The Truth About the First Amendment

The plain and overwhelming burden of the evidence is that the First Amendment, like the Constitution, grew out of a markedly (though that is not to say perfectly!) Christian society; that it was intended to prevent the creation and the evils of a national established church; that it was intended to guarantee religious freedom, but not to sanction license in the name of liberty; and that it was intended to protect and preserve the rights of "religious" people in general, and particularly of Christians, as full citizens of the American republic. The truth is that the First Amendment was intended to protect the religious liberty of all who adhere to basically biblical standards of ethics and morals, not of those who would practice immorality in the name of religious liberty.[17] The truth is that the First Amendment was intended to protect the right of Christians to continue to influence, and even to dominate, our national civil government, public life and law.

> *The people and statesmen who gave us the First Amendment ... wanted a separation of church and state without a separation of Christianity and civil government, law, or public life.*

The people and statesmen who gave us the First Amendment did not want a union of church and state in the sense of a national established church. But neither did they want to divorce Christianity from our national counsels, fundamental law, or laws made pursuant to the Constitution. They wanted a separation of church and state at the national level, but not necessarily at the state level: for the First Amendment spoke only to the

Inauguration of Washington in City Hall. Engraving. © Bettmann/CORBIS

national government and left the states to continue to make their own settlements regarding the relationship of Christianity to their civil governments and laws. They wanted a separation of church and state without a separation of Christianity and civil government, law or public life. That is the truth about the First Amendment.

Church and State: The Federal Record

There is far more evidence of the intended relationship between "church" (religion or Christianity) and "state" (our national government) than summarized above. That evidence is found at the level of our national government. It consists in the many kinds of connections between Christianity and our central government, from the time of the inauguration of George Washington, our first president, until well into the twentieth century. It consists of many kinds of actions by our representatives and statesmen in our national government. It consists not in the actions of a carefully selected few individuals, but rather in the actions of a multitude of our elected and appointed officials in the national government. It consists not in what a few of these men said or wrote when they were old and long out of the sphere of public accountability, but in the actions and words of our statesmen when they were in public office.

The evidence of the federal record is not now publicly known, but that is because it has not been taught to the public—not that it is difficult to teach. It is rather easy to know and to teach. Nor is its meaning arcane; indeed, it is rather easy to understand and interpret. It has not been taught to the public for at least these reasons:

- Christians have become ignorant of its existence.
- Christians have not had a view of the world and of life, including a view of civil government as a ministry of God (Romans 13) which values the biblical duty of Christians to be salt and light to the society around them and to obey godly standards of law.
- Christians have let non-Christian and anti-Christian ways of thinking come to dominate our educational, cultural and governmental institutions.
- Non-Christian thought is not neutral, but instead is opposed to the theological and often also to the ethical principles of the Bible and Christianity.
- Adherents of non-Christian religious philosophies have worked diligently for many decades to de-Christianize our educational institutions, civil government, law and public life, and the de-Christianization of these things requires an eradication of the knowledge of the influence of Christianity upon our civil government, law and public life.

Although these things are so, the federal record has not been destroyed. It can be salvaged, studied, and put to constructive uses in the cause of God and Truth. One primary use is a restoration of the true understanding of the purposes of the First Amendment and of the intended place of Christianity ("religion") in the law and public life of our country. A knowledge of the place of honor which our earlier American representatives and statesmen gave to Christianity and Christian principles is of immeasurable value to present and future generations of Americans. Such an invaluable knowledge can be gained from a consideration of the following summary of the evidence of the federal record.[18]

Actions of the First Congress

Nothing makes the purpose of the First Amendment clearer, and at the same time more soundly refutes the claims of the neutralists and secularists, than the call of the First Congress on September 25, 1789—the very day it had completed its work on what would become the First Amendment—for a national day of prayer and thanksgiving. The First Congress resolved that a joint committee of both Houses of Congress request the President to recommend to the people of these United States a day of public thanksgiving and prayer, to be observed by acknowledging, with grateful hearts, the many signal favors of Almighty God, especially by affording them an opportunity peaceably to establish a Constitution of government for their safety and happiness.[19]

Only one congressman, Rep. Thomas Tucker of South Carolina, opposed the resolution. The ground of his opposition was that the resolution was "a religious matter and, as such, is proscribed to" Congress.[20] Neither James Madison (who is often alleged to have been a proponent of "absolute separation" of Christianity and civil government) nor anyone else supported Tucker's position.

Note well that the resolution was not directed to express thanks to "Nothing" (the atheist position of secularism), nor "To Whom It May Concern" (the agnostic position of secularism), nor to "Any and All Gods Worshipped by Men" (the "religious neutralist" position). Rather, this overwhelmingly Christian, predominantly Protestant Congress sought, with grateful hearts, a day of public thanksgiving and prayer to be directed to "Almighty God": it intended that thanks be given to the God acknowledged by Christians to be the only true God, the Creator and providential Ruler and Judge of Heaven and Earth.

The First Congress made a Christian worship service part of President Washington's inauguration.

Some time before it debated what would become the First Amendment, the First Congress made a Christian worship service part of President Washington's inauguration. By concurrent resolutions, the United States Senate, on April 27, 1789, and the United States House of Representatives, on April 29, 1789, made a divine service part of the very first presidential inauguration under the Constitution and the new national government. This official service was conducted by the Right Reverend Samuel Provost, who had been elected Chaplain of Congress on April 29, 1789. The service was held in St. Paul's Chapel, an Episcopal church. The President, the Vice-President, and all the members of the House and the Senate attended the service. Washington solemnly took his oath of office, kissed the Bible upon which he had placed his hand while the oath had been administered,[21] and read his obviously Christian inaugural address. No one voiced any objections about the plainly Christian nature of the inaugural ceremonies and the action of Congress.

The Congress of the United States did not undergo a religious and philosophical revolution between the end of April 1789 and the months of August and September 1789, when it debated what became the First Amendment. For after it finished debating what became the First Amendment, Congress debated whether to grant an exemption from military service to Quakers and members of other pacifistic Christian denominations. It did not include adherents of other recognized religions—much less adherents to the dogmas of secularist philosophies or ideologies—in its deliberations. In other words, Congress acted just as if it had not created a religiously "neutral" or a secularist First Amendment. Congress acted as if it had not de-Christianized our fundamental law—just as it was to do when it requested a presidential proclamation of a national day of thanksgiving and prayer to Almighty God.

Of course, the First Congress did other "unneutral," "non-secularist," plainly "religious" things. The First Congress reenacted the Northwest Territories Ordinance of 1787, with its once-famous call for the promotion of religion, morality and knowledge in 1789. In fact, the First Congress reenacted the Northwest Territories Ordinance, with tellingly providential timing, on the very day Congress finished its work on the First Amendment! This Congress also established a system of congressional chaplains and a system of military chaplains.

The First Congress acted just as if it intended to maintain and preserve an essential connection between Christianity and our national government and law.

The truth is that the First Congress repeatedly acted as if it had not intended our national government, law and public life to be either "religiously neutral" or secularist. The First Congress acted just as if it intended to maintain and preserve an essential connection between Christianity and our national government and law. The pattern established by the First Congress was, of course, followed by subsequent Congresses—without any congressional expressions of fear that the First Amendment was being violated, because they knew that the First Amendment was not being violated by such actions.

Presidential Inaugural Addresses

The continuing connection between Christianity and our national government is also readily visible in American presidential inaugural addresses. From Washington's First Inaugural Address on, the inaugural addresses of all of our presidents—whether or not they were Christians—refer respectfully to God, or to God's divine providence and to our nation's and the president's dependence upon Him.

For example, President John Adams, replying to a resolution of both House and Senate, said, in his "Inaugural Address" (1797):

> … if a love of virtuous men of all parties and denominations; if a love of science and letters and a wish to patronize every rational effort to encourage schools, colleges, universities, academies, and every institution for propagating knowledge, virtue and religion among all classes of the people, not only for their benign influence on the happiness of life in all its forms, but as the only means of preserving our Constitution from its natural enemies, the spirit of sophistry, the spirit of party, the spirit of intrigue, the profligacy of corruption, and the pestilence of foreign influence, which is the angel of destruction to elective governments; if a love of equal laws, of justice, and humanity in the interior administration; … if a veneration for the religion of a people who call themselves Christians and a fixed resolution to consider a decent respect for Christianity among the best recommendations for the public office can enable me in any degree to comply with your wishes, it shall be my strenuous endeavor that this sagacious injunction of the two Houses shall not be without effect.

Adams praised Christianity—and only Christianity. He made it clear that a decent respect for Christianity—not a lowering of Christianity to a status of equality with all other religions of man, and certainly not a denigration of Christianity by forbidding it to influence civil government and the making of law—is an excellent qualification for public office, particularly among a people who profess to be Christians. As the Northwest Ordinance had done, Adams publicly linked "religion" (Christianity), virtue and knowledge and favored the propagation of the three. And as Washington had done the previous year in his "Farewell Address," Adams made it clear that "religion" (Christianity) is essential to the preservation of our Constitution and therefore also of equal laws, justice and liberty.

Jefferson, like Washington and Adams, gave public encouragement to Christianity.

Thomas Jefferson's "First Inaugural Address" (1801) did not signal a revolutionary turn to secularism or religious neutrality. Instead, Jefferson, like Washington and Adams, gave public encouragement to Christianity and to Christian morality. Describing the situation of the United States in that day, he said:

> ... enlightened by a benign religion professed, indeed, and practiced in various forms, yet all of them inculcating honesty, truth, temperance, gratitude, and the love of man; acknowledging and adoring an overruling Providence, which by all its dispensations proves that it delights in the happiness of man here and his greater happiness hereafter—with all these blessings, what more is necessary to make us a happy and prosperous people? Still one thing more, fellow citizens—a wise and frugal Government, which shall restrain men from injuring one another, shall leave them otherwise free to regulate their own pursuits of industry and improvement, and shall not take from the mouth of labor the bread it has earned. This is the sum of good government, and this is necessary to close the circle of our felicities.

The religion to which Jefferson referred was, of course, Christianity: no other religion comes close to fitting his description of religion in America in 1801. Like his wise predecessors, he did not accept the notion that America's national happiness and prosperity could or would be produced by any and all religions of man or by secularism.

Even Jefferson's once-famous (because once-taught) delineation of "the sum of good government" was plainly compatible with the biblical teaching of Romans 13, with the Golden Rule, and with the prohibition against covetousness and theft in God's law. And Jefferson's well-phrased expression of these principles would have been seen by his audience of early Americans to have been quite consistent with the benign religion which most of them professed and which so many of them, via their various denominations, practiced.

Clearly, Jefferson's "First Inaugural Address" was neither "neutral" among all religions nor secularist. Like the addresses of his great predecessors in the American presidency, Jefferson's address rejected secularist and "neutralist" notions of the First Amendment. Like them, Jefferson here recognized at least something of the theological, philosophical, ethical, legal and political importance of Christianity to American liberty, morality, prosperity and justice.

The truth is, as Charles LaFontaine has noted, American presidential inaugural addresses, from the time of Washington to at least the time of James Buchanan,

> revealed a definite, fixed canon of ideas concerning God, the nation, and their interrelationship. In the classical form, the Divine Being appears under various titles as the Supreme Ruler of the world in which universal laws have been divinely established. Human beings, regardless of their religion or its lack, must obey these laws to the peril of their individual good and the world's general welfare. Obedience to law brings divine favor which is reflected in creaturely happiness, success and prosperity; disobedience effects quite the opposite. Yet the deity is far more involved with human beings than in merely dispensing rewards and punishments. The Divine Being is actively engaged in the history which human beings are making. Indeed, the deity actually relates to them in a contractual manner.[22]

The biblical nature of this "classical form" of American presidential inaugural address is unmistakable. The rhetorical tradition of presidential inaugural addresses stressed the idea that the United States is a covenanted nation, a chosen people of God, with an important role in His eternal plan for world history. Hence, Americans, the tradition held, are to be a light to the nations, "an example to others of divine qualities like justice, peace and freedom."[23] Just as Deuteronomy 28, the passage to which the Bible was so often opened when the oath of office was given to our presidents, teaches so forcefully covenantal faithfulness by man—faith in God and obedience to His laws—brings God's blessings on the nation, while covenantal unfaithfulness—disobedience—brings God's judgments on the nation.[24] These principles are fully consistent with the covenantal nature of the state constitutions, declarations of rights, and bills of rights. They are also consistent with the rhetorical teaching of the many public political sermons and lectures to which Americans had long been accustomed in conjunction with elections and other functions of their state and local governments.

These obviously Christian references to God and to His relationship with the American nation were quite consistent with preserving a connection between Christianity and the functioning of our national government—without the creation of a national established church and without infringing the religious liberty of American citizens. These references were, of course, inconsistent with either religious "neutrality" or secularism.

Presidential Addresses and Messages

Presidents did not abandon Christian rhetoric after their inaugural addresses were delivered. They did not then sound atheistic, agnostic or religiously "neutral" notes. On the contrary, they continued the "religious" rhetoric of their inaugural addresses in their other public speeches. In their annual messages to Congress and in other addresses, American presidents continued to acknowledge the importance of God's divine providence—His sovereign intervention in and direction of history, including the life of the nation. They acknowledged their (and the nation's) dependence upon God. They directed Americans' gratitude for national peace, liberty and prosperity to God. And they instructed Americans that humiliation and repentance are our proper responses to the difficulties that God brings upon us for our sins. Perhaps the greatest of the addresses and messages delivered by an American president is Washington's once-famous "Farewell Address" (1796). Ratification of the First Amendment certainly did not prevent our first President from giving official encouragement to "religion" in his "Farewell Address," for in taking his leave of our nation's highest elective office, Washington emphasized the crucial importance of "religion" to our national well-being and liberty:

> Of all the dispositions and habits which lead to political prosperity, religion and morality are indispensable supports. In vain would that man claim the tribute of patriotism who would labor to subvert these great pillars of human happiness—these firmest props of the duties of men and citizens. The mere politician, equally with the pious man, ought to respect and cherish them. A volume could not trace all their connections with private and public felicity. Let it be simply asked, Where is the security for property, for reputation, for life, if the sense of religious obligation desert the oaths which are the instruments of investigation in courts of justice? And let us with caution indulge the supposition that morality can be maintained without religion. Whatever may be conceded to the influence of refined education on minds of peculiar structure, reason and experience both forbid us to expect that national morality can prevail in exclusion of religious principle.

Our first President clearly and forcefully rejected the notion of some secularists that religion and morality are antithetical to human

Our first President clearly and forcefully rejected the notion of some secularists that religion and morality are antithetical to human happiness, liberty, justice, and political prosperity.

happiness, liberty, justice and political prosperity. This great President also rejected the notion of other secularists that religion and morality bear little or no relationship to these things. Like the overwhelming majority of his fellow American citizens, gentlemen and statesmen, Washington knew that religion and morality are absolutely essential to human happiness, political prosperity, justice and liberty. He knew that without religion and morality there would be no security for reputation, property and life itself, and political prosperity, justice and liberty would be lost, along with human happiness. Like many of his fellow statesmen, Washington said publicly and privately that this was so. Unlike many lesser men and less-informed minds, Washington knew that the connections between religion, morality, and public and private felicity are vast and complicated as well as essential and inseparable. He indicated their complexity—and simultaneously encouraged people to devote study and thought to this crucially important subject—by stating that a volume could not trace all the connections of religion (Christianity) and morality with public and private happiness.

So strong was Washington's conviction on this subject that he denied that one who works to subvert religion and morality can be termed, or legitimately claim, the tribute of being known as a patriot.

It cannot honestly be supposed that Washington was praising religion in general, nor all religions and their respective moral systems. For Washington was well known for his Christian piety and moral rectitude: he was a Christian, not a Baha'i. Furthermore, Washington was not so ignorant of the religions of man as to be unaware that diverse non-Christian religions require actions which are abhorrent to Christian morality, and so also to reputation, property, life, liberty and justice.[25]

Most presidential messages and addresses were not so notable as Washington's "Farewell Address." Nor were most of them pronouncements that would whet the appetite of theologians. Yet these other official presidential addresses were not theologically "neutral," and they were surely not secularist. They, too, gave official presidential recognition to God, to His authoritative role in history, and to His intimate involvement in the affairs of the American nation. They, too, reveal no notion that the presidents who delivered them were violating the First Amendment.

Presidential and Other Oaths of Office

Presidential and other oaths of office are one with our tradition of presidential addresses in manifesting a clear connection between Christianity and our national government, law and public life. The United States Constitution requires the president-elect to take an oath (or, for those who believe that the Bible forbids one to take an oath, affirmation) of office. It also prescribes the form and content of this oath (or affirmation):

> I do solemnly swear (or affirm) that I will faithfully execute the Office of President of the United States, and will to the best of my Ability, preserve, protect, and defend the Constitution of the United States.

The given form of the oath does not mention God or Jesus Christ, yet this is not evidence of secularism or religious neutrality. For it was well known at the time of the framing and ratification of the Constitution that in the very act of swearing to or affirming an oath, one directs one's promises to God. Hence, it was well known that in the act of swearing or affirming his oath of office, the president was directing his promises to preserve, protect and defend the Constitution to God.[26] Furthermore, in swearing to preserve, protect and defend the Constitution of the United States, the president-elect is declaring his intention to protect and preserve a Constitution which is laden with Christian principles of ethics and law. Moreover, he is swearing before God to preserve, protect and defend a Constitution which itself affirms, in its seventh article, that Jesus Christ is Lord.[27]

The fact that the oath of office was seen as being made before— under the authority of—God was made unmistakably clear by the establishment of the custom of having the president swear his oath (or make his affirmation) of office with his hand upon the Bible. The custom was initiated by the committee which planned the first inauguration: the committee decided that Washington should take his oath with his hand placed on a Bible. This is a custom, not a constitutional requirement. But it is a telling custom, for it points to the source of authority about God and to the nature of the God under whose authority the president-elect promises to preserve, protect and defend the Constitution.

Since Washington took that first oath of office, every president who has participated in a public inauguration or swearing-in ceremony has done so with his hand placed upon a Bible. Theodore Roosevelt was the only President who did not have his hand placed upon a Bible when he took the oath of office, but this was because there was not a Bible in the house in which he was given the oath after the death of President William McKinley.[28]

The ties of Christianity to our central government were underscored by another precious tradition begun by Washington, who added the words, "So help me, God" to the end of his oath. With the exception of Theodore Roosevelt, who took his oath in a private or semiprivate ceremony, every president has concluded his inaugural oath with these non-secularist, non-religiously neutral words.

Although most American presidents have been Christians,[29] even the few non-Christian presidents have adhered to this tradition established by Washington. Why did the few non-Christian presidents adhere to this tradition? Why did such men as Jefferson, for whom this was not a long-established practice, and who is supposed to have been so dead-set against giving any public, governmental support to "religion" or Christianity, follow the lead of Washington in this matter? And why did such as Fillmore and Taft, who, like Jefferson, were essentially Unitarians,[30] continue the traditional practice?

The answer to these questions is at least twofold. First, these presidents recognized that they were being inaugurated into an office established by a Christian people. Second, these presidents knew that this long-established American practice did not and does not violate the intentions behind the First Amendment.

So manifest was the fact that the legal and civil government institutions of the United States were established by and for an overwhelmingly Christian people that as late as 1892 the United States Supreme Court, in *Church of the Holy Trinity v. United States* (143 U.S. 457), noted that the form of oath which universally prevailed in the United States in the 1890s concluded with an appeal to the Almighty. This indicates plainly that the tradition begun by Washington was not

> *The custom of concluding the presidential oath of office with the words, "So help me, God" became a tradition because of the manifest religious, moral, and political dominance of Christianity in the nation.*

established simply, or mainly, because of the prestige of one man, even though he be so great as Washington. The custom of concluding the presidential oath of office with the words, "So help me, God" became a tradition because of the manifest religious, moral and political dominance of Christianity in the nation.

This is true of another custom begun when Washington kissed the Bible after completing his oath. This is an indication of the devout piety of Washington. But the action became a custom because it is highly appropriate for men who love the revealed Word of God (and because it is a useful action for men who want to seem to love the Bible in a nation which is dominated by people who profess to believe and esteem the Bible as the revealed Word of God). The action is symbolically fitting for the chief executive of a national government which has been established by such a people.

On less celebrated levels of American civil government and public life, what has been said about the presidential oath of office could be said about the oaths of office taken by the vice-president, by senators and by congressmen. The same could even be said of the oaths of office taken by federal judges and by U.S. Supreme Court justices. All holders of these federal government offices swear, after all, to uphold—not to rewrite, subvert or overthrow!—the Constitution. Their oaths, too, grow out of the beliefs, traditions, professions and aspirations of the American people who gave us the Constitution. Their oaths, too, are implicitly directed to God, not merely to the American people whom they represent.

Presidential Proclamations

Presidential proclamations of days of humiliation, fasting and prayer (in times of difficulty) or of thanksgiving (in good times) are another powerful evidence of the continuing connection between Christianity and our national government. Such proclamations were usually issued at the request of Congress—in response to a congressional resolution—so they were really the work of congressional majorities (routinely overwhelming majorities), not simply of presidents.

The eminently biblical practice of issuing such proclamations dates back to at least the time of Puritan New England. It was followed by both the various state governments and the Continental Congress during our War for Independence. The Continental Congress recommended numerous such days to the chief executives of the state governments during the movement for independence.

Even Thomas Jefferson (who always acknowledged the providence of God in national affairs) recommended, as a member of the Virginia House of Burgesses, the observation of a day of fasting and prayer upon receiving news of the Boston Port Bill of July 1774. The Virginia legislature agreed. Washington sent a special message to his family and constituents to observe the day. George Mason admonished his household to keep the day strictly and to wear the garb of mourning to church.

Whether they were made at the state or the national level, these proclamations were emphatically Christian. They are precisely the opposite of a desire to separate Christianity from American civil government on any level, and of a desire to make American civil government "neutral" among all religions.[31]

Probably the most telling of these proclamations is the recommendation made by the First Congress to President Washington that a day of thanksgiving and prayer be celebrated by the people of the new nation. Congressman Elias Boudinot, the Christian statesman who had chaired the Committee of the Whole which first considered the First Amendment, recommended such a day of thanksgiving and prayer because he would not think of letting the session of Congress pass without giving all the citizens of the United States an opportunity to join in "returning to Almighty God their sincere thanks for the many blessings He had poured down upon them."[32]

It is particularly telling that this recommendation by Congress was made on September 25, 1789, just after the House had finished debating what became the First Amendment and on the same day the Senate passed the final version of what became the First Amendment. Obviously, neither the members of the House nor the members of the Senate saw any violation of the proposed amendment in their passage of this very God-centered resolution. Nor did President Washington believe that any violation of the proposed amendment was involved in the proclamation of a national day of thanksgiving to Almighty God. The great President promptly complied with the Congress' request, recommending that a day of thanksgiving should be celebrated on February 19, 1790.[33]

Robert Cord, a fine student of the religious aspect of the First Amendment, notes that this first thanksgiving proclamation set a precedent which became a custom:

> The precedent set by the request of the First Congress for
> a national day of Thanksgiving and Washington's

proclamation of 1789 became a custom during the early life of the new Federal Republic. Of our first presidents— those closest to the Constitutional Convention and the adoption of the First Amendment—George Washington issued at least two such proclamations calling for a day of "public thanksgiving and prayer." John Adams issued at least two, and James Madison issued at least four. There is no evidence that any of these men believed they were violating the Federal Constitution, including the First Amendment, and consequently their oath of office, in issuing these proclamations during their presidencies.[34]

It is important to note that President Adams' two proclamations were for days of fasting and prayer, and that his first proclamation contained emphatically Trinitarian Christian affirmations. It is very important to note that President Madison's proclamations of days of prayer and fasting also contained clearly Christian statements.[35]

Thomas Jefferson was the only one of our first presidents who did not make such proclamations and publicly stated his belief that the Constitution and the First Amendment forbade such actions by the central government. Yet this does not prove he believed that the "Establishment Clause" of the First Amendment requires a complete separation of religion from civil government, for (as shall be seen below in more detail) Jefferson's own actions as president refute such a notion. Three times he signed into law congressional extensions of a 1796 act which, in effect, gave federal aid to Christian Indians in the western lands, thereby working to spread Christianity among the Indians. In 1803 President Jefferson approved a treaty with the Kaskaskia Indians; the treaty had the effect of providing federal government support to the work of the Roman Catholic Church among the Indians.[36] If he had believed that the First Amendment and its "Establishment Clause" required a complete separation of religion from civil government, he would not have supported any legislation or treaty which involved the provision of federal aid to the dissemination of Christianity among the Indians. Jefferson supported such legislation and such a treaty because he did not believe that either the First Amendment or the "Establishment Clause" forbids federal government aid to the promotion of Christianity. Nor did he believe that the First Amendment or the "Establishment Clause" requires a complete separation of religion and civil government.

But the issue does not revolve around the beliefs and actions of

Jefferson. For not only Presidents Washington, Adams and Madison, but also presidents as late as John Tyler (1841), Zachary Taylor (1849), James Buchanan (1860), and Abraham Lincoln (1861) issued proclamations of national days of fasting and prayer on appropriate occasions. The Jefferson of the secularists was certainly "outvoted" by these other American presidents.

Clearly, the tradition of presidential proclamations of national days of humiliation, fasting and prayer, or of national days of thanksgiving and prayer, declares that the vast majority of our presidents—and of the Congresses who recommended the observance of such days—believed that such actions by the federal government are consistent with the First Amendment and its "Establishment Clause."

Jefferson and Madison in Office

It is important, for several reasons, to consider the actions of Thomas Jefferson and James Madison when they were in public office. Jefferson and Madison are often misinterpreted as advocates of a complete separation of "religion" (Christianity) from civil government, law and public life. They are also misrepresented as having believed that the First Amendment (or its "Establishment Clause") requires a complete separation of "religion" (Christianity) from American central government, law and public life. And these supposed opinions of Jefferson and Madison are inaccurately said to be representative of the views on the relationship between religion and civil government of the statesmen who gave us the Constitution, the Bill of Rights, and the First Amendment.

This is a study of the actual intentions of the statesmen who gave us the First Amendment (and its "Establishment Clause"), and not a study of theoretically possible relationships between religion and civil government in the abstract. Since this is so, it is important that the actions of Jefferson and Madison when they were in public office—not when they were old and long removed from public office and public accountability for their views and actions—be considered. Their views decades after they had retired from public life are of theoretical interest, but are irrelevant to the question of the intentions behind the First Amendment, precisely because their later views were expressed when they were private citizens, not elected representatives of the American people who could be chastised for such views by the electorate. Moreover, their later views were not necessarily the same as the views that they held when they were in elected office. Madison's views of the

Jefferson and Madison had different views on the relationship between "church and state." But what they did when they were in public office was, on the whole, clearly supportive of Christianity.

relationship between religious liberty and public life changed after he was old and out of public office.[37] As Robert Cord has convincingly shown, it is what Jefferson and Madison did when they were in public office and accountable to the public which must be the criterion for determining what they really thought about the meaning of the First Amendment's religion clauses. What they did when they were in public office is entirely different from the historically fictional account of their views given by secularist theorists and propagandists.[38]

Jefferson and Madison had different views on the relationship between "church and state."[39] But what they did when they were in public office was, on the whole, clearly supportive of Christianity.

Jefferson was not a Deist (a believer in a "watchmaker-God" who created the universe but does not intervene in its working) but rather what would be called a Unitarian. And at that he was a secret Unitarian, not an open one. A member of the vestry of his local Anglican church, he never wrote for public consumption anything against Christianity. He composed his infamous "Jefferson Bible," a Bible with all references to the miracles of Christ and all of Christ's claims to divinity excised, but kept it secret. Far from seeking to undermine Christianity, he publicly professed his belief in fundamental tenets of Christianity via his words and actions. He contributed freely to the building of Christian churches, to Bible societies, to other "religious" endeavors, and to the support of the clergy. All of his important early state papers, including the Declaration of Independence, contain clear references to God and His providence, or to Christianity. Similar religious references are visible in his inaugural addresses and in many of his annual presidential messages. In these official public statements he refers to God in ways that Christians could accept as the God who reveals Himself in the Bible, declares that he believes in the efficacy of prayer, says that it is a duty to praise God as the Author of all mercies, and (as his "First Inaugural Address" makes clear) praises the Christian religion of the people of the United States.[40]

Though Jefferson and Madison worked for the disestablishment of their own Anglican Church in Virginia, that disestablishment did not produce a de-Christianization of the laws of Virginia. Nor did their role in revising the Virginia legal code produce a de-Christianization (via secularism or religious "neutrality") of the laws of their state. As Daniel L. Dreisbach has shown, contrary to secularist scholars' and Supreme Court justices' misinterpretations, none of the five religion bills which Jefferson and Madison supported as part of the revision of the Virginia legal code—not even the famous "Bill for Establishing Religious Freedom"—mandated a separation of "religion" (Christianity) from Virginia law. In fact, the other four neglected bills—which accompanied and directly followed Jefferson's "Bill for Establishing Religious Freedom," Bill No. 82—unmistakably gave Christianity the support of Virginia law. Bill No. 83 provided for saving the property of the formerly established Anglican Church. Bill No. 84 was entitled, "A Bill for Punishing Disturbers of Religious Worship and Sabbath Breakers." Bill No. 85 was entitled, "A Bill for Appointing Days of Public Fasting and Thanksgiving." Bill No. 86 tied the authority of the Bible directly to the definition of marriage in Virginia. It was entitled, "A Bill Annulling Marriages Prohibited by the Levitical Law, and Appointing the Mode of Solemnizing Lawful Marriage." Obviously, secularist "scholars" and Supreme Court justices who have appealed to Jefferson's celebrated "Bill for Establishing Religious Freedom" as an argument for the secularization and de-Christianization of American law have, to say the least, seriously misinterpreted the views of Jefferson and Madison on "church and state." The actions of Jefferson and Madison in revising the Virginia legal code are no precedent for a religiously "neutral" or a secularist First Amendment. Far from de-Christianizing Virginia law, these bills continued the connection between Christianity and the laws of the Old Dominion.[41]

As President of the United States, Jefferson did some things which—when isolated from his other actions as President and interpreted in a certain way—can be used to support the notion that he sought to divorce "religion" from our national public life. In 1802 he wrote the famous letter to the Danbury Baptist Association, in which, opposing Thanksgiving Day proclamations, he claimed that the First Amendment established "a wall of separation between church and state." He made no Thanksgiving Day proclamations. He opposed national days of prayer. Yet these actions by Jefferson are an insufficient foundation for a claim that he sought to secularize American law and public life.

Actually, President Jefferson also took a number of official actions which supported Christianity. He certainly used Christian rhetoric in his inaugural and other presidential addresses. In his "Second Inaugural Address" (1805), Jefferson told his hearers that we are in the hands of the God who

> ... led our fathers, as Israel of old, from their native land and planted them in a country flowing with all the necessaries and comforts of life; who has covered our infancy with His providence and our riper years with His wisdom and power, and to whose goodness I ask you to join in supplications with me that He will so enlighten the minds of your servants, guide their councils, and prosper their measures that whatsoever they do shall result in your good, and shall secure to you the peace, friendship and approbation of all nations.

There was no secularist "wall of separation" in such presidential rhetoric!

In addition, while Jefferson was superintendent of schools for Washington, D.C., those schools—in accordance with his plan for them—used the Bible and Isaac Watts' great Protestant Hymnal as textbooks. As was the case with Congress' reenactments of the Northwest Territories Ordinance, Jefferson's plan for using these great books as textbooks for the schools of the District of Columbia recognized the connection between Christianity, morality and knowledge which was then well known to be fundamental to educational excellence.

As we have seen, President Jefferson also recommended and signed treaties which gave federal government money to support a Roman Catholic priest in his priestly duties, to help build a Roman Catholic church, and to allow the Indians to use federal money to support Christianity among themselves. He also signed into law three extensions of a 1796 act (in 1802, 1803 and 1804) which helped Christian Indians to propagate Christianity among the heathen Indians.[42] And while President, Jefferson attended Christian worship services in the halls of Congress. Obviously, there was no "religiously neutral" or secularist "wall of separation" in such actions, but there was support of Christianity by the federal government.

President Jefferson attended Christian worship services in the halls of Congress.

Similarly, the actions of James Madison when he was in public office reveal no "wall of separation" between Christianity or "religion" and the central government. This Christian statesman did help to "disestablish" his own Anglican Church in Virginia, but that disestablishment was not intended to bring about the de-Christianization of Virginia law and did not do so. Moreover, Madison's famous "Memorial and Remonstrance against Religious Assessments," which was so influential in the struggle for disestablishment in his state, was neither secularist nor "religiously neutral." On the contrary, this usually selectively-quoted document was in reality a plea by Christian statesmen to Christian statesmen—a plea which looked forward to the triumph of Christianity over all other religions of man throughout the world. And Madison's argument in the "Memorial and Remonstrance" was that disestablishment and rejection of taxes imposed to support Christian ministers would be good for liberty and for Christianity.

Madison joined Jefferson in revision of the Virginia legal code. But, as we have seen, their revisions (and proposed revisions) of that code certainly did not remove the connection between Christianity and Virginia law. Instead, these revisions clearly maintained the connection between Christianity and Virginia's laws.

In the Constitutional Convention, Madison made no "religious neutrality" or secularist protests against the inclusion of an obviously Christian reference, in Article VII, to the year in which the Constitution was completed: "the year of our Lord one thousand, seven hundred eighty-seven ..."

In the First Congress, Madison opposed both a national established church and the states' established churches. Contrary to the standard misinterpretations of Madison's role in the debates over the First Amendment, Madison did not dominate the debates. He saw his purpose basically triumph in regard to the national established church, because virtually nobody in Congress wanted to have a national established church. He saw his purpose in regard to the states' established churches defeated because most members of the First Congress wanted to leave the states—as the First Amendment was to leave them—free to make their own settlements regarding the relationship between religion and civil government.

The principles which Madison set forth as the reasons for his (and the House committee's) introduction of a proposed Bill of Rights were consistent with maintaining a connection between Christianity and the central government—but not with the philosophy of "religious neutrality" nor with the philosophy of secularism.[43]

And Madison's arguments in the First Congress during the debates on what became the First Amendment supported neither "religious neutrality" nor secularism, even though he had ample opportunities to espouse either philosophy during the debates.[44]

In the First Congress, Madison also participated in—and did not oppose—the creation of the system of chaplains for Congress and the system of chaplains for United States military organizations. He also voted for the House's call to President Washington to proclaim a national day of thanksgiving to God for the success of the establishment of our new system of national government under the Constitution.

As president, Madison made no less than four proclamations of national days of prayer and thanksgiving to God. To be sure, Congress had requested that he make these proclamations. But President Madison did not have to make these proclamations if he did not want to. He could have made an issue of the matter, but he did not. As president, Madison made these highly "unneutral," anti-secularist proclamations of national days of thanksgiving to God.

This evidence indicates quite clearly that neither Jefferson nor Madison, while in public office, really held to a notion of "neutrality" among all religions, much less to a notion of secularism as a constitutional mandate. The actions of neither man support the long predominant notion that the "Establishment Clause" of the First Amendment requires a separation of Christianity from our civil government and law.

The System of Congressional Chaplains

Even if the actions of Jefferson and Madison when they were in public office had been different, it should be obvious that their actions alone are insufficient to make a case that our early statesmen thought that the First Amendment requires "neutrality" among all religions or secularism as the standard for our national law. For it is obvious that Jefferson and Madison were but two of the many statesmen who participated in the framing and ratification of the Constitution and the Bill of Rights (Jefferson, of course, participated in neither, since he was in France at the time) and the operation of our new national government during the early decades of its existence. Those other statesmen far outnumbered Jefferson and Madison. Collectively, they were far, far more influential than Jefferson and Madison. Even if what we are usually told about Jefferson's and Madison's views concerning "church and state" were true—and they are not—the views and actions about "church and state" of this far greater body of statesmen and representatives far outweigh those of Jefferson and Madison.

One of the many unmistakably Christian things this far greater body of statesmen did was to establish the system of Congressional chaplains. In the very first Congress, Oliver Ellsworth, a Christian statesman, was appointed by the Senate to confer with a committee of the House about "rules and the appointment of chaplains." The House chose five Christian statesmen—Elias Boudinot, Theodoric Bland, James Madison, Roger Sherman, and Thomas Tucker—to serve on this committee. The result was that each house purposely appointed a chaplain of a different Christian denomination: the Senate appointed an Episcopal clergyman and the House appointed a Presbyterian minister. By this means, Christianity was supported by the national government without the danger of establishing any one denomination as the official church of our nation.

This process began a practice which has continued ever since. Furthermore, in the early decades of the Republic, the chaplains who were appointed to these Congressionally authorized posts were among the most outstanding clergymen of their day: they were Christian clergymen who were known for their character as well as for their ability to preach and pray.

Madison, of course, was a member of the committee which made the successful recommendation that a system of chaplains be established for the Congress of the United States. This is significant, for Madison—who is falsely claimed to have been an advocate of "religious neutrality" or of secularism—raised no objection to the creation of the chaplaincy system. Instead, he helped to create it! Madison had no objection to this obvious endorsement of Christianity by our national government, so long as Christianity was represented by men from a variety of denominations.

Systems of Military Chaplains

Following a tradition which dated back before the War for Independence and a Biblical principle and practice which is traceable to Deuteronomy 20:2-4, the First Congress also established systems of chaplains for American military and naval forces. This was a principle and practice of all Christian nations at the time.

The exercise of this principle had been most evident in our War for Independence, for the clergy had been among the leaders of the independence movement, and many were leaders in the war effort.

Many of the military units sent to combat by the various states during the war had chaplains. Washington, who would lead worship services himself if no chaplain were present, had urged the Continental Congress to appoint one chaplain for each regiment. Congress had appointed chaplains for the army, the navy and hospitals. Many of these chaplains were outstanding for their learning, eloquence and piety, as well as for their courage. Many earned distinction in theological literature, in education and in science, as well as in the pulpit.

Very early, the House of Representatives, and then the Senate, authorized the use of their halls in the Capitol for weekly religious worship services.

Here, too, the First Congress—and subsequent Congresses, which, of course, continued the practice—gave federal government support, including money, to Christianity.

Christian Services in the Capitol

Instead of seeking to separate "religion" (Christianity) from our national government, both houses of Congress gave unmistakable support to Christianity in another significant way. Very early, the House of Representatives, and then the Senate, authorized the use of their halls in the Capitol for weekly religious worship services.

These were, of course, Christian religious services. In these services, the United States Marine Corps Band, which attended in uniform, played the psalms and other music which were sung in worship to the Lord. Invitations to preach in these services were extended by Congress' chaplains, who often preached to the assembled federal government officials and citizens themselves. Preachers from orthodox Protestant churches, as well as Quakers and Roman Catholics, were invited to preach at these services.[45] Obviously, such services involved the support of the central government for "religion," and not merely for "religion" in general.

Tellingly, the Capitol was used for Christian religious services during the administration of Thomas Jefferson. Neither Jefferson nor Madison protested against the conduct of such Christian religious services in the halls of Congress. In fact, both of these supposedly "absolute separationist" presidents frequently attended such services.[46]

Use of the Capitol for Sunday worship services apparently declined during the 1850s, but the practice revived during the difficult years of the War Between the States. In the aftermath of the great war, however, the custom again declined. Although as late as 1847, before the war, John Hughes, Archbishop of New York, had delivered an address in the Capitol on "Christianity, the Only Source of Moral, Social and Political Regeneration," by the late 1880s there were no more Sabbath services in the Capitol. Apparently the custom quietly ceased, without any open congressional debate or public notice.[47] Nor was the cessation of this Christian custom accompanied by any pronouncement that the practice had violated "separation of church and state" or any supposed constitutional principle of "religious neutrality" or secularism.

Treaties

The treaties approved by the central government offer another kind of evidence of the continuing connection between Christianity and our national government. Many of these treaties were achieved via the active participation of the president. All of them, of course, had the constitutionally-required approval of at least two-thirds of the members of the United States Senate. By way of these treaties, the central government gave its sanction to the support of "religion"—that is, Christianity.

Propagandists of the secularist theory of the First Amendment love to claim that the 1797 treaty with Tripoli contained a denial that the government of the United States "is … in any sense, founded on the Christian religion.…"

In making such a claim, they apply their common tactic of taking a quotation out of its context. This doubtful clause supposedly proves that America was not a Christian nation and that Christianity was intended to be separated from the conduct of our national government. Of course, they divorce this alleged clause of the treaty from the great mass of evidence which is summarized in this essay. Then they do not inform us that this treaty, supposedly translated by Joel Barlow, an anti-Christian rationalist who was then the American consul in Algiers, was replaced by a new treaty (1805) which did not contain this alleged clause. In effect, the second treaty repudiated the alleged anti-Christian lie of the first treaty.

But there is a darker side to this matter. The English translation of the 1797 treaty with Tripoli is badly distorted from the Arabic text. Joel Barlow oversaw the translation of the treaty into English. In Article 12 of Barlow's version of the treaty, all religious references in the Arabic were removed. Moreover, the original Arabic contained no such article as the infamous Article 11 of Barlow's "translation"—the very article which contains the clause which the secularizers love to quote: "the government of the United States of America is not in any sense founded on the Christian religion...." This much-publicized article does not exist at all in the original Arabic of the 1797 treaty![48]

The treaties that the secularists and "religious neutrality" theorists neglect provide even stronger evidence of the continuing support of Christianity by our central government, long after the ratification of the First Amendment.

Less than five years after the ratification of the First Amendment, the Washington administration negotiated a treaty (1795) with the Oneida, Tuscarora and Stockbridge Indians. In this treaty the United States agreed to pay $1,000 to build a church at Oneida to replace the one which the British had destroyed during the War for Independence.

Jefferson's treaty with the Kaskaskia Indians resulted in hundreds of federal government dollars being given to the Indians to be used for various Christian religious purposes. This money was to be used on lands which, according to the treaty, became part of the United States. This neglected treaty was signed in 1803—the year after Jefferson's infamous letter to the Danbury Baptist Association, the letter in which his "wall of separation between church and state" quote appears.

President James Monroe—Madison's former Secretary of State—negotiated a treaty with the Wyandots and other Indian tribes; this treaty guaranteed United States land to the rector of the Roman Catholic Church of St. Anne in Detroit and to the College of Detroit, because the Indians were Roman Catholics.

John Quincy Adams (Monroe's former Secretary of State) signed a treaty with the Osage and other Indian tribes (1825) which provided for a "missionary establishment" on ceded U.S. land to be "employed in teaching and civilizing and improving the said Indians."

Andrew Jackson did not issue Thanksgiving Day proclamations, because he thought they violated the "Establishment Clause." Yet he signed a treaty with the Kickapoo Indians (1833) which required the United States government to pay $3,700 to build a mill and a church.

Martin Van Buren signed a treaty with the Oneida Indians (1838) in which the United States government paid for the construction of a church and a parsonage.

It is also well worth noting that the unmistakably Christian designation of time, "the year of our Lord ...," was commonly used in treaties between the United States and the various Indian tribes. Interestingly, this Christian designation of time was often used in such treaties signed during and after the administration of Thomas Jefferson.[49]

Neither the presidents nor the two-thirds (and greater) majorities of the United States Senate which approved these treaties thought they were being either unconstitutional or unfair to the other religions of the world in enacting such treaties. Clearly, they did not seek to separate Christianity from the conduct of our national government, nor did they seek to maintain a strict "neutrality" among all religions of the world in negotiating and approving these treaties. Obviously, in supporting Christian construction and missionary activity in or among these Indian tribes, our presidents and Senate majorities were, in fact, promoting Christianity and opposing the various pagan religions or forms of unbelief that were present among the Indians involved in the treaties.

Obviously, in supporting Christian construction and missionary activity in or among these Indian tribes, our presidents and Senate majorities were, in fact, promoting Christianity and opposing the various pagan religions or forms of unbelief that were present among the Indians involved in the treaties.

These American presidents and two-thirds Senate majorities knew that their actions supporting the work of various Christian denominations among the Indians did not constitute an "establishment of religion" for the nation. None of these treaties required all American citizens—or even all Indians who were parties to the treaties—to join a particular Christian denomination, to proclaim belief in its creed, to attend its worship services, to pay it taxes, or to conform to any other requirements of the established churches with which these presidents' and legislators' forefathers had been familiar in England and Europe before their migration to America. It is safe to say that none of these presidents or legislators wanted to create such an established church for our nation. At the same time, none of them saw anything unconstitutional or immoral about giving central government support to preserving and promoting the influence of Christianity and Christian civilization among the Indians.

Federal Support of Christian Education to Civilize the Indians

It was not only by federal treaties that the central government gave support to the advancement of Christianity among the Indians. For by routine congressional action and presidential approval, our federal government spent money annually to support Christian missionaries, schools and religious teaching for the purpose of civilizing the Indians.

Robert Cord says of this longstanding federal government activity:

> In fact, under the guise of bringing "Civilization to the Indians," many United States Congresses and presidents provided hundreds of thousands of dollars of federal money for more than a century, to support ministers of many religions, missionaries, and religious schools which, I am sure none dispute, might have taught "just a bit" of religion along with reading, writing and Western culture.[50]

The many "religions" to which Cord refers were, in fact, not "religions," but various Christian denominations. The teachers could not have truly taught Western culture to the Indians without teaching them more than "just a bit" of "religion," or Christianity, for Christianity is the very foundation, and to a large extent, the content of Western culture. Furthermore, the federal government's intent to bring civilization to the Indians was not a guise, but rather a genuine concern, as evidenced by the financial outlay and the duration of such activities. Moreover, the expenditure of federal funds to support teachers of various Christian denominations in these educational activities indicates that, rather than seeing the bringing of civilization to the Indians by means of giving them a Christian education as a "guise," these congressional majorities and presidents identified Christianity and civilization. They identified Christianity and civilization because they identified Christianity, morality, and the kinds of knowledge upon which civilization, in general, and the civilization which they valued, in particular, is based.

The commitment of Congresses and presidents to civilizing and Christianizing the Indians can be partly measured by the sums expended. In March, 1819, for instance, Congress appropriated $10,000 to be given to the missions boards of many Christian denominations for work among the Indians. John C. Calhoun, in his capacity as Secretary of War, gave thousands of dollars to the missions societies from 1817 to 1825 to aid their Christianization and education of the Indians. Federal government funds were given to all the main denominations—Congregationalist, Baptist, Presbyterian, Methodist, Episcopal, Moravian and Roman Catholic—through the 1830s and beyond, for the purpose of educating the Indians. By 1896,

Congress was annually appropriating more than $500,000—a lot of money, in gold or silver—to support Indian education carried on by various Christian denominations' organizations.[51]

In 1897 this longstanding practice was terminated by a congressional decision to stop appropriating money for education in any "sectarian" school. But this was merely a change in policy, not a decision that previous policy had been in violation of the Constitution.[52] This new policy was not motivated by secularism. If this new policy was motivated by "neutrality," it was a neutrality among Christian denominations, not a "neutrality" among all religions.

Reenactment of the Northwest Ordinance

The 1789 reenactment of the Northwest Ordinance of 1787 is a particularly telling example of another kind of federal government support of "religion." At the same time, it shows our early statesmen's concern for Christianizing and civilizing both the Indians and the non-Indians in the states of the old Northwest Territories.

The "Ordinance for the Government of the United States Northwest of the River Ohio" had been actively promoted by George Washington. It had been modeled on the Massachusetts Constitution—a beautifully Christian document—and had been only slightly revised on its way through Congress. Its purpose was "the prevention of crime and injuries, and for the execution of process, criminal and civil." It established the familiar pattern of New England township government for the new states that would be created out of these territories.[53] The Northwest Ordinance was definitely concerned with "religion." Its first article guaranteed religious liberty, proclaiming that "No person, demeaning himself in a peaceable manner, shall ever be molested on account of his mode of worship or religious sentiments."[54] It is evident that "a peaceable and orderly manner" of one's demeanor during his religious activities was conceived by the statesmen who supported this law as being conduct according to Christian standards of peaceableness and orderliness. This is made plain by the fact that the third article of the Northwest Ordinance began with these important words:

> Religion, morality, and knowledge being necessary to good government and the happiness of mankind, schools and the means of education shall forever be encouraged.[55]

These words from this act simply expressed the common knowledge of American statesmen of that day—a knowledge virtually lost to today's politicians—that "religion" is essential to the maintenance of morality, which in turn is essential to man's individual and social happiness as well as to good government. As the act's own language makes clear, the concern was to promote good government, in general. Since it was common in that day to distinguish between civil government and other kinds of government—self-government, family government, church government, etc.—it is reasonable to conclude that the authors of the act, who knew the importance of "religion" to virtue, and of virtue to good government, were concerned to promote the success of all kinds of government—via the promotion of "religion," morality and knowledge. This is unmistakably clear, since the very next sentence in the law required that:

> The utmost good faith shall always be observed toward the Indians; their lands and property shall never be taken from them without their consent; and in their property, rights and liberty, they never shall be invaded or disturbed.[56]

The authors of these words saw education based on religion and morality as essential to prevent settlers in the Northwest Territories, under or apart from the authority and action of civil government, from dealing unjustly with the Indians.

Far from seeing "religion," morality and knowledge as separated, the act's authors saw them, as did educators, legal theorists and political thinkers of that time—as intimately linked. Education which combined "religion" and morality would tend to produce the individual self-government, family government and civil government which would be conducive to virtuous (by preventing or restraining vicious) conduct between whites and Indians, as well as among whites.

The kind of education promoted by this act was seen as being necessarily and inseparably tied to "religion." This religion was not "religion" in the abstract. It was, of course, Christianity. Christianity had overwhelmingly infused and directed American education in that day, and at all levels gave to American education its rationale as well as its content. Neither ethics nor knowledge were separated from "religion" in the American schools and colleges of the time.[57] It was quite normal then for the statesmen who framed the Northwest Ordinance to take for granted the link between Christianity, morality and education. And it was quite "natural" for them to provide for the

Neither ethics nor knowledge were separated from "religion" in the American schools and colleges of the time. It was quite normal then for the statesmen who framed the Northwest Ordinance to take for granted the link between Christianity, morality, and education.

same basic sort of education which they had received, and which the great majority of Americans were still receiving, in their arrangements for this important region which would eventually become new states in the Federal Union. These legislators sought to encourage settlers in the Northwest Territory to "train-up" their God-given children in the way they should go.

The enabling legislation for the Northwest Ordinance stipulated that section sixteen in each township was to be "given perpetually for the purposes contained in the said Ordinance," that is, for "religion, morality and knowledge," the ends for which the school was to be established in each township. This law also required that section twenty-nine of each township "be given perpetually for the purposes of religion," so that churches could be established and pastors' salaries paid.[58] Not only federal rhetoric but also federal financial aid—to the tune of the profits from two square miles (two sections of 640 acres each) of federal land—were to be given to aid "religion."

The gift of this federal land and the purposes for which the schools supported by it were forever to be encouraged were, in effect, a federal subsidy for the promotion of Christian education, the Christian religion, and Christian morality. The subsidy was quite consistent with the federal government policy of supporting Christian missionary and educational work among the various Indian tribes which were to be encountered on the frontier. The "civilization" and Christianization (the two were virtually equated in such federal laws) of some of the wilder folk on the frontier was a continuing concern of many people back East, as well, no doubt, as of many of the more civilized, Christianized settlers on the frontier. The promotion of Christianity and Christian morality among the Indians was seen to be important to the spread of Christian civilization and to the peace and good government which Christian civilization entails. So, also, the promotion of Christianity and of Christian morality among the settlers of the West was seen as important to the fulfillment of these ends.

The framing and ratification of the new Constitution, and later of the First Amendment, did not make the Northwest Ordinance a dead letter. During the summer of 1787, when the Constitution was being framed, Congress three times used the Ordinance and its enabling legislation in the sale of western lands. The third use occurred after the Constitutional Convention. The Ordinance and its enabling legislation were also used (more or less) in 1790, when North Carolina ceded Tennessee to the United States; in 1800, when Congress divided the Northwest Territory into two governmental units; and in 1802 (the year of Jefferson's letter to the Danbury Baptist Association), when Congress required Ohio's constitution and laws to conform to the Ordinance. In addition, the principles of the Ordinance were recognized by the Ohio legislature when it chartered that state's first university. Significantly, under Madison's administration, in 1809, Congress specifically applied all the requirements of the Ordinance to the territory of Illinois. The same occurred (with certain reservations) under President Monroe in 1817; in 1819, when Alabama entered the Union; in 1836, when Wisconsin applied for statehood; and in 1848, when Oregon became a territory.[59] So the religious and educational principles of the old Northwest Ordinance continued to be in force until the middle of the nineteenth century.

Dedication Ceremonies of Federal Buildings

The ceremonies dedicating the national Capital, the District of Columbia, and various federal government buildings in it provide further evidence of the continuing close ties between Christianity and our central government after the ratification of the First Amendment. The District of Columbia was set apart by Congress on July 16, 1790. Its first cornerstone was fixed at Jones's Point, near Alexandria, on April 15, 1791, "with all the Masonic ceremonies usual at that time, and a quaint address, almost all in scriptural language, delivered by the Rev. James Muir."[60]

On September 18, 1793, the southeast corner of the Capitol itself was laid by President Washington, "with Masonic and Christian services" and military demonstrations.[61]

On November 25, 1800, the first Congress to occupy the new Capitol opened its session. President John Adams addressed the assembled legislators with some unabashedly "religious" words:

> It would be unbecoming the representatives of this nation to assemble for the first time in this solemn temple without looking up to the Supreme Ruler of the universe and imploring his blessing.... May this territory be the residence of virtue and happiness! In this city may that piety and virtue, that wisdom and magnanimity, that constancy and self-government, which adorned the great character whose name it bears, be forever held in veneration! Here, and throughout our country, may simple manners, pure morals and true religion forever flourish.[62]

The Senate replied to the President with equally "religious" remarks:
Impressed with the important truth that the hearts of rulers and people are in the hands of the Almighty, the Senate of the United States most cordially joins in your invocations for appropriate blessings upon the Government and people of this Union....[63]
Referring to the recent death of George Washington, the Senate continued:

> ... We derive consolation from the belief that, in the moment we were destined to experience it, the loss we deplore was fixed by that Being whose counsels cannot err, and from a hope that, since in this seat of government which bears his name and his earthly remains will be deposited, the members of this Congress, and all who inhabit the city, with these memorials before them, will retain his virtues in lively recollection and make his patriotism, morals and piety for imitation.

> We deprecate with you, sir, all spirit of innovation, from whatever source it may rise, which may impair the sacred bond that connects the different parts of this empire; and we trust that, under the protection of Divine Providence, the wisdom and virtue of the citizens of the United States will deliver our national compact, unimpaired, to a grateful posterity.[64]

President Adams assented to the Senate's words, replying in kind. The "true religion" and "pure morals" which he (and they) wished would "forever flourish" there were none other than those of Christianity, as both his speeches on this public occasion and his other public addresses indicate. The "piety" and "morals" to which both his speeches and those of the Senate referred on this quite public occasion were those of Washington: Christian piety and morals, not those of any other religion. Nor is it too much to infer that the President and the Senate would have opposed "innovations" which would impair the sacred bond of the nation with the God whose divine providence they mutually acknowledged in these public exchanges.

After the Capitol was enlarged, the building's new cornerstone was laid by President Fillmore on July 4, 1851, before a huge audience. Beneath this cornerstone was deposited a memorial composed by Daniel Webster, the Christian statesman and great orator who was then Secretary of State. Among other things, Webster's statement expressed the conviction that:

> ... all here assembled, whether belonging to public life or to private life, with hearts devoutly thankful to Almighty God for the preservation of the liberty and happiness of the country, unite in the sincere and fervent prayer that this deposit, and the walls and arches, domes and towers, the columns and entablatures, now to be erected over it, may endure forever![65]

Webster's dedicatory address emphasized that:

> ... the strong and deep-settled conviction of all intelligent persons among us is that, in order to preserve this inheritance of liberty and to support a useful and wise government, the general education of the people and the wide diffusion of pure morality and true religion are indispensable. Individual virtue is a part of public virtue. It is difficult to conceive how there can remain morality in the government when it shall cease to exist among the people or how the aggregate of the political institutions, all the organs of which consist only of men, should be wise and beneficent and competent to inspire confidence, if the opposite qualities belong to the individuals who constitute those organs and make up the aggregate.[66]

The "pure morality and true religion" which this Christian statesman—together with the great majority of his hearers—considered to be "indispensable" were Christian morality and religion.

This cornerstone, like the two previously noted, was laid with a combination of Christian and Masonic ceremonies.[67] Yet it is a mistake to take this as anything more than a certain syncretism and lack of discernment on the part of many Americans of the day. For British and American Freemasonry, in contrast to Continental Freemasonry, was not motivated by either anti-Christian or revolutionary sentiments. Although Masonry's secret teachings about God were syncretistic and unbiblical, these teachings were not for popular consumption, even within the organization, but were reserved for members of the higher orders of the organization. Apparently in its American version, Masonry's teachings were vague enough so that many American Christians saw nothing un-Christian about enjoying the fellowship to be found in their local societies of Masons. It was for these reasons that Washington and many other Protestants, as well as Thomas Fitzsimmons of Pennsylvania and Daniel Carroll of Maryland, the two Roman Catholics who helped frame the Constitution, were Masons.[68]

Clearly, the combination of Masonry and Christianity in such ceremonies was not secularist. Nor, despite the syncretism of Masonic teachings about God, was the combination of Christianity and Masonry in such ceremonies intended to imply an equality of all religions or moralities. Even Masonry did not teach the equality of all concepts of God, nor of all religions. Besides, Christianity was the ruling element in such combinations and public ceremonies, through the peculiar variety of Masonry which existed on these shores, and particularly through the manifest Christianity of the addresses delivered by statesmen like Webster at such public ceremonies. No public place was given to any other religion.

The dedication of the cornerstone of the Washington Monument provides another important symbolic illustration of this truth. This cornerstone was laid on July 4, 1848, in the presence of the President, other statesmen, and a large throng of citizens. Robert C. Winthrop, Speaker of the House of Representatives, in a commemorative address on George Washington, traced our first President's "exalted goodness and greatness to the influence of the Christian religion."[69] Then the Rev. J. McJilton gave a long, eloquent prayer, which included the following powerful words:

> And now, O Lord of all power and majesty, we humbly beseech Thee to let the wing of Thy protection be ever outspread over the land of Washington! May his people be Thy people! May his God be their God! Never from beneath the strong arm of Thy providence may they be removed; but, like their honored chief, may they acknowledge Thee in peace and in war, and ever serve Thee with a willing, faithful acceptable service! Hear our prayer, we beseech Thee, that the glory of this nation may never be obscured in the gloom of guilt; that its beauty may never be so marred by the foul impress of sin that the light of its religious character shall be dimmed. Open the eyes of the people, and let them see that it is their true interest to study Thy laws, to seek Thy favor, and to worship Thee with a faithful worship.... All these mercies and blessings we ask in the name and mediation of Jesus Christ, our most blessed Lord and Savior. Amen.[70]

There can be no mistaking the "religious" nature of such a ceremony, nor of such a prayer!

Christian Signs and Symbols on and in Federal Government Edifices

Christian signs and symbols on the Capitol, the Washington Monument, and other public edifices of the federal government provide further testimony of the pervasive public influence of Christianity in the early Republic. B.F. Morris, a great student of the subject, said in 1863:

> The paintings and statuary which adorn the rotunda and the halls of Congress are all suggestive symbols of scenes in the history of our Christian civilization and of the triumph of our principles of civil liberty and government. The nine large paintings in the rotunda represent DeSoto's Discovery of the Mississippi, the Landing of the Pilgrims at Delft, the Landing of the Pilgrims at Plymouth Rock, the Signing of the Declaration of Independence, the Surrender of Burgoyne at Saratoga, the Surrender of Cornwallis at Yorktown, and the Resignation of

Washington at Annapolis. Groups of sculpture, representing scenes in our early Christian history and in the westward march of civilization, adorn the various parts of the Capitol, whilst similar symbols suggest Christian ideas and scenes on the eastern portico....[71]

Gary DeMar provides a more up-to-date list of examples of pronouncements that signify our nation's Christian commitment. Among them are:

- The words "In God We Trust" are inscribed in the House and Senate chambers.
- On the walls of the Capitol dome, these words appear: "The New Testament according to the Lord and Savior Jesus Christ."
- In the Rotunda is the figure of the crucified Christ.
- The Latin phrase *Annuit Coeptis*, "[God] has smiled on our undertaking," is inscribed on the Great Seal of the United States.
- Under the Seal is the phrase from Lincoln's Gettysburg Address: "This nation under God."
- President Eliot of Harvard chose Micah 6:8 for the walls of the Library of Congress: "He hath shown thee, O man, what is good; and what doth the Lord require of thee, but to do justly, and to love mercy, and to walk humbly with thy God?" (KJV).
- The lawmakers' library quotes the psalmist's acknowledgement of the beauty and order of creation: "The heavens declare the glory of God, and the firmament showeth His handiwork" (Psalm 19:1 KJV).
- Engraved on the metal cap on the top of the Washington Monument are the words: "Praise be to God." Lining the walls of the stairwell are numerous Bible verses: "Search the Scriptures" (John 5:39 KJV), "Holiness to the Lord," and "Train up a child in the way he should go, and when he is old he will not depart from it" (Proverbs 22:6 KJV).
- The crier who opens each session of the Supreme Court closes with the words, "God save the United States and this Honorable Court."
- At the opposite end of the Lincoln Memorial, words and phrases from Lincoln's second inaugural address allude to "God," the "Bible," "providence," "the Almighty," and "divine attributes."

- A plaque in the Dirksen Office Building has the words "IN GOD WE TRUST" in bronze relief.
- The Ten Commandments hang over the Supreme Court bench.[72]

The Christian signs and symbols adorning these edifices, together with the Christian public ceremonies with which these federal buildings and monuments were dedicated, provide abundant, manifest, inescapable evidence of the continuing public connection between Christianity and our national government.

The Traditional Prayer Opening Each Session of the U.S. Supreme Court

Since at least 1947, secularist Supreme Court majorities have waged a relentless attack on the Christian nature and principles of our fundamental law. Thus it can be said figuratively as well as literally that the Ten Commandments hang over the head of the Chief Justice of the Supreme Court and, by extension, over the heads of all of these officials, who are known as "justices." Yet the deeply rooted Christianity of our land has even been traditionally recognized in the custom of announcing the opening of a session of the United States Supreme Court.

It can be said figuratively as well as literally that the Ten Commandments hang over the head of the Chief Justice of the Supreme Court.

Although the use of a Christian prayer to open each session of the Supreme Court is not expressly stipulated in the Constitution, the traditional opening of the marshal of the Court rings loud and clear to those who have ears to hear:

> Oyez! Oyez!! Oyez!!!
>
> All persons having business before the Honorable, the Supreme Court of the United States, are admonished to draw near and give their attention, for the court is now sitting.
>
> God save the United States and this Honorable Court![73]

Given the lawless and irresponsible behavior of Supreme Court majorities over the past five or six decades—particularly in regard to misinterpretation of the First Amendment, protection of the lives of pre-born and newborn babies, and violation of the intentions of the Framers and Ratifiers of the Constitution, the Bill of Rights, and other amendments—there is considerable irony in this prayer. Yet irony or no irony, even so simple a thing as this traditional prayer, which is intimately connected to the forms and procedures of the Court, testifies to the manifest connection between Christianity and the functioning of our central government. For the prayer itself acknowledges both the Authority under which the Court (and the central government) operates and the providential nature of God.

The fact that the prayer is neither explicitly prescribed in the Constitution nor mandated by federal law is beside the point. For surely the significant fact is that this custom has become traditional and has so long persisted without a formal legal basis.

Obviously, the prayer became traditional precisely because it was and is consistent with the Christian religious commitment and ethics of our people and with the Christian foundation and content of our Constitution, Bill of Rights, and laws.

Let it be duly and clearly noted that the plea of this prayer is not for the aid of Allah, the blessings of Buddha, or the vengeance of Vishnu. Much less is the plea directed to the mere reason, science or intuition of man; or to the people of the nation, of an ethnic group, of a race, or of the entire world. The plea is directed to none other than God, just as is the traditional English plea for the monarch: "God save the king!" This is fitting for a Supreme Court over whose heads the Ten Commandments, by appropriate and telling custom, hang. Moreover, it is quite appropriate, under a Constitution which was framed and ratified by overwhelmingly Christian groups of men representing distinctly Christian states, and which implicitly acknowledges the lordship of Christ, for the nation's highest Court—which is constitutionally required (in Article VI) to swear an oath or make an affirmation to support the Constitution—to be opened with so serious a plea to God for the nation and for its highest Court. This, too, is evidence of Christianity, not of "religious neutrality," nor of secularism at the highest levels of the federal government.

Federal Judges' Decisions

Federal judges' decisions and learned jurists' commentaries repeatedly reaffirmed the Christianity of our people and laws well into the twentieth century. The United States Supreme Court, in the *Girard Will* case (1844) expressly said that Christianity is part of the Common Law of Pennsylvania. In addition, the Court implied that Christianity is so intimately connected with the civil institutions of the United States that provisions of a will inconsistent with the Christian religion would not have been protected by the authority of the United States government.[74] The legal conflicts of the United States with the Mormon Church, upholding federal laws against polygamy and federal government disposition of the confiscated property of members of the Mormon community, reaffirmed the basic Christianity of our nation and its laws. Speaking for the Supreme Court in its denial of the "right" of polygamous marriage, Chief Justice Waite said:

> Laws are made for the government of actions, and while they cannot interfere with mere religious belief and opinions, they may with religious practices. Suppose one believed that human sacrifices were a necessary part of religious worship, would it be seriously contended that the civil government under which he lived could not interfere to prevent a sacrifice? Or, if a wife religiously believed it was her duty to burn herself upon the funeral pile of her dead husband, would it be beyond the power of the civil government to prevent her carrying her belief into practice? So here, as a law of the organization of society under the exclusive dominion of the United States, it is provided that plural marriages shall not be allowed.[75]

As R. Kemp Morton notes in this connection, "that part of the law of the land which forbade polygamy was the customs of a Christian people become law."[76]

A few years later Justice Bradley, speaking for the Supreme Court in its decision against the Mormon Church in the property case, proclaimed:

> The organization of a community for the spread and practice of polygamy is, in a measure, a return to barbarism. It is contrary to the spirit of Christianity and of the civilization which Christianity had produced in the Western world.[77]

As Morton has said, the teaching of the Supreme Court in the Mormon cases was clear:

> The Mormon Church and the world at large were to learn that the Constitution of the United States was not a pagan political document and that the First Amendment to the Constitution was not a cloak for practices—even religious

practices—profaning the moral ideals of a Christian people. More than this, they were to learn that in a Christian country there could be an unlawful exercise of worship when the tenets of a sect either permitted or directed conduct contrary to the tenets of Christianity.[78]

> *The Supreme Court recognized that the "free exercise of religion" in a Christian country like the United States does not permit violations of Christian standards of ethics.*

In other words, the Supreme Court recognized that the "free exercise of religion" in a Christian country like the United States does not permit violations of Christian standards of ethics.

As late as 1933, there had been no federal court dissent from, or qualifications of the views of the United States Supreme Court expressed by Justice Brewer in Rector, etc., of *Holy Trinity Church v. United States* (1892):

> … no purpose of action against religion can be imputed to any legislation, state or national, because this is a religious people. This is historically true. From the discovery of this continent to the present hour, there is a single voice making this affirmation.…

If we pass beyond these matters to a view of American life as expressed by its laws, its business, its customs, and its society, we find everywhere a clear recognition of the same truth. Among other matters, note the following: The form of oath universally prevailing, concluding with an appeal to the Almighty; the custom of opening sessions of all deliberative bodies and most conventions with prayer; prefatory words of all wills, "In the name of God, Amen"; the laws respecting the observance of the Sabbath, with general cessation of all secular business, and the closing of courts, legislatures, and other similar public assemblies on that day; the churches and church organizations which abound in every city, town and hamlet; the multitude of charitable organizations existing everywhere under Christian auspices; the gigantic missionary associations, with general support, and aiming to establish Christian missions in every quarter of the globe. These, and many other matters which might be noticed, add a volume of unofficial declarations to the mass of organic utterances that this is a Christian nation.[79]

In 1933, before the destructive impact of anti-Christian

presuppositions and thinking on our federal courts had become manifest, a learned lawyer summarized American courts' decisions regarding Christianity:

> The judges have said that we must regard the people for whom our law was ordained; that our constitutions show on their face that the Christian religion was the religion of their Framers; that whatever is irreligious in the most instances is wrong and in many instances it is illegal; that Christianity is so involved in our social nature that even those among us who reject it cannot possibly get clear of its influence or reject those customs and principles which it has spread among our people, so that like the air which we breathe they have become the common stock of the whole country and essential elements of its life....
>
> We find then that, whether in the realm of judge-made law where those who sit on the wool sack of our appellate courts interpret and apply the customs of our people, or whether in the interpretation of statutes prohibiting blasphemy or prohibiting work and labor on Sunday, or dealing with the marriage relation or with moral issues, our courts have spoken with one voice and in universal recognition of the place of Christianity in the law of the land.[80]

The "Liberal" Attack

Revealing evidence of the pervasive influence of Christianity upon American civil governments, law and public life is contained in the program of the National Liberal League. Basing its argument on the false premises that (1) "natural morals," the desires of the "natural man," are a sufficient basis for the order, prosperity and happiness of a "secular" society, and (2) the Constitution was neither founded upon nor intended to preserve Christian values, the "Liberal League" called for a virtual legal revolution in American public life:

1. We demand that churches and other ecclesiastical property shall no longer be exempted from just taxation.
2. We demand that the employment of chaplains in Congress, in State Legislatures, in the navy and militia, and in prisons, asylums, and all

other institutions supported by public money, shall be discontinued.

3. We demand that all public appropriations for sectarian, educational and charitable institutions shall cease.

4. We demand that all religious services now sustained by the Government shall be abolished and especially that the use of the Bible in the public schools, whether ostensibly as a text-book or avowedly as a book of religious worship, shall be prohibited.

5. We demand that the appointment by the President of the United States, or by the Governors of the various States, of all religious festivals and fasts shall wholly cease.

6. We demand that the judicial oath in the courts and in all other departments of the Government shall be abolished, and that simple affirmation under the pains and penalties of perjury shall be established in its stead.

7. We demand that all laws, directly or indirectly enforcing the observance of Sunday as the Sabbath, shall be repealed.

8. We demand that all laws looking to the enforcement of "Christian" morality shall be abrogated, and that all laws shall be conformed to the requirements of natural morality, equal rights and impartial liberty.

9. We demand that not only the Constitutions of the United States and of the several States, but also in the practical administration of the same, no privilege or advantage shall be conceded to Christianity or any other special religion: that our entire political system shall be founded and administered on a purely secular basis and that whatever changes shall prove necessary to this end shall be consistently, unflinchingly and promptly made.[81]

Even if one does not take the atheistic and agnostic nature of the leadership of the National Liberal League to indicate the root of the "liberals'" demands on our constitutions, civil governments and laws, the very nature and timing of the "liberal" demands is telling. For these demands were made not in the mid-twentieth century, but in the early 1870s. So deep and pervasive were the connections between Christianity and our civil governments—emphatically including the central government—that the "liberals" of the 1870s were compelled by their secularist desires to demand an irreligious revamping of "our entire political system," in order to refound it and administer it "on a purely secular basis." In the very act of demanding that our civil governments, laws and constitutions be secularized, they were compelled to testify to the many kinds of connections that existed between Christianity and all levels of our civil governments.

Some, being informed of this, might argue that the connections between Christianity and our civil governments, laws and public life existed because Christians "took over" our civil governments after the revivals of the 1800s. But such an argument would not be borne out by history. For, as the evidence sketched above indicates, the evidence concerning the framing and ratification of the Constitution, the Bill of Rights, and the First Amendment points to the intention to maintain connections between Christianity and our central government, while avoiding the problems associated with a national established church. And the massive evidence of the many kinds of connections between Christianity and our central government (particularly when taken with that of the connections between Christianity and our state governments) summarized above makes it clear that these connections existed before the framing and ratification of the First Amendment, as well as from the beginning of our new national government. Though Christianity was undoubtedly strengthened, in some ways, by the revivals of the early 1800s, Christians did not have to "take over" the central government because it had already been founded on Christian principles and was already in the hands of a predominantly Christian group of statesmen.

The Verdict of the Federal Record

The evidence of the federal record of the relationship between "church and state"—Christianity and our central government—is massive, unmistakable and conclusive. With devastating authority, it refutes secularist and "religious pluralist" notions of the intended meaning of the religion clauses of the First Amendment. It conclusively and overwhelmingly establishes the truth that the First Amendment was not intended to separate Christianity from our fundamental law and national (much less state and local) government, or to make Christianity the legal equal of all other religions. If either of these false alternatives had been the intention of the Framers and Ratifiers of the Constitution and the First Amendment, then this huge, neglected body of evidence would not exist.

The voluminous federal record exists because the vast majority of early American presidents, senators, congressmen, and judges agreed that the conjunction of Christianity and our fundamental law and public life is both constitutional and good. No honest evaluation of the evidence of the federal record can lead to any other verdict or conclusion.

Notes

[1] Archie P. Jones, *Christianity in the Constitution: The Intended Meaning of the Religion Clauses of the First Amendment* (Ph.D. dissertation, University of Dallas, 1991; available from U.M.I., 300 North Zeeb Road, Ann Arbor, Michigan 48106), 1-477; Chester James Antieau, Arthur T. Downey, and Edward C. Roberts, *Freedom from Federal Establishment: Formation and Early History of the First Amendment's Religion Clauses* (Milwaukee: Bruce Publishing Co., 1964); Sanford H. Cobb, *The Rise of Religious Liberty in America* (New York: Cooper Square Publishers, [1902] 1968); Isaac A. Cornelison, *The Relation of Religion to Civil Government in the United States of America: A State Without a Church But Not Without a Religion* (New York: Da Capo Press, [1895] 1970); Robert L. Cord, *Separation of Church and State: Historical Fact and Current Fiction* (New York: Lambeth Press, 1982); Norman DeJonge and Jack Van Der Slik, *Separation of Church and State: The Myth Revisited* (Jordan Station, Ontario: Paideia Press, 1985); Daniel L. Dreisbach, *Real Threat and Mere Shadow: Religious Liberty and the First Amendment* (Westchester, Illinois: Crossway Books, 1987); John Eidsmoe, *Christianity and the Constitution* (Grand Rapids: Baker Book House, 1987); Tim LaHaye, *Faith of Our Founding Fathers* (Brentwood, Tennessee: Wolgemuth and Hyatt, Publishers, 1987); James McClellan, "The Making and Unmaking of the Establishment Clause," in McGuigan and Rader, eds., *A Blueprint for Judicial Reform* (Washington, D.C.: Free Congress Research and Education Foundation, 1981), 295-324; B. F. Morris, *Christian Life and Character of the Constitution of the United States, Developed in the Official and Historical Annals of the Republic* (Philadelphia: George W. Childs, 1864); R. Kemp Morton, *God in the Constitution* (Nashville: Cokesbury Press, 1933); A. James Reichley, *Religion in American Public Life* (Washington, D.C.: The Brookings Institution, 1985); Anson Phelps Stokes, *Church and State in the United States*, 3 vols. (New York: Harper and Brothers, 1950); John W. Whitehead, *The Separation Illusion: A Lawyer Examines the First Amendment* (Milford, Michigan: Mott Media, 1977); Mark de Wolfe Howe, *The Garden and the Wilderness: Religion and Government in American Constitutional History* (Chicago: University of Chicago Press, 1965); Steven Alan Samson, *Crossed Swords: Church and State in American History* (Ph.D. Dissertation, University of Oregon, 1984).

[2] For a logical and chronological account of the formation of the "religion clauses" and the First Amendment in the First Congress, see Jones, *Christianity in the Constitution*, 478-653.

[3] The classic scholarly work in this camp is Anson Phelps Stokes, *Church and State in the United States*, 3 vols. (New York: Harper and Brothers, 1950). A fatal flaw of Stokes' work and position is that the massive evidence of the connections between "religion" and our national government and other civil governments which he presents is overwhelmingly evidence of connections between Christianity and these civil governments, not of a desire to be neutral among all the religions of man. The most that can be said of the evidence presented by Stokes is that the statesmen who gave us the First Amendment intended to provide religious freedom to all whose religions do not violate basically biblical standards of ethics.

[4] Leonard Levy, *The Establishment Clause: Religion and the First Amendment* (New York: Macmillan, 1986); Thomas J. Curry, *The First Freedoms: Church and State in America to the Passage of the First Amendment* (New York: Oxford University Press, 1986); Leo Pfeffer, *Church, State and Freedom* (Boston: Beacon Press, 1953), and *God, Caesar, and the Constitution: The Court as Referee of Church-State Confrontation* (Boston: Beacon Press, 1975); Irving Brant, *The Bill of Rights: Its Origin and Meaning* (Indianapolis: Bobbs-Merrill Co., 1965).

[5] Patricia U. Bonomi, *Under the Cope of Heaven: Religion, Society and Politics in*

Early America (New York: Oxford University Press, 1986).

⁶Jones, *Christianity in the Constitution*, 79-144.

⁷Jones, *Christianity in the Constitution*, 145-230.

⁸Ellis Sandoz, *A Government of Laws: Political Theory, Religion and the American Founding* (Baton Rouge: Louisiana State University Press, 1990); Ellis Sandoz, ed., Political Sermons of the American Founding Era, 1750-1805 (Indianapolis: Liberty Press, 1991); see also Eidsmoe, *Christianity and the Constitution*.

⁹Donald S. Lutz and Charles S. Hyneman, "The Relative Influence of European Political Writers on Late Eighteenth-Century American Political Thought," *American Political Science Review* 189 (1984), 189-197; see also Eidsmoe, *Christianity and the Constitution*.

¹⁰Jones, *Christianity in the Constitution*, 339-477; Archie P. Jones, *Christianity and Our Early State Constitutions, Declarations and Bills of Rights*; Parts I and II (Plymouth, Massachusetts: Plymouth Rock Foundation, 1994); Wilber G. Katz, *Religion and the American Constitutions* (Evanston, Illinois: Northwestern University Press, 1964); and Stephen Botein, "Religious Dimensions of the Early American State," in Richard Beeman, Stephen Botein, and Edward C. Carter, eds., *Beyond Confederation: Origins of the Constitution and American National Identity* (Chapel Hill: University of North Carolina Press, 1987), 315-330.

¹¹Jones, *Christianity in the Constitution*, 395-477.

¹²See M.E. Bradford, *A Worthy Company: Brief Lives of the Framers of the Constitution* (Plymouth, Massachusetts: Plymouth Rock Foundation, 1982); M.E. Bradford, *Religion and the Framers: The Biographical Evidence* (Plymouth, Massachusetts: Plymouth Rock Foundation, 1993).

¹³Jones, *Christianity in the Constitution*, 231-287; see also Archie P. Jones, *Christian Principles in the Constitution and the Bill of Rights*; Parts I and II (Plymouth, Massachusetts: Plymouth Rock Foundation, 1994).

¹⁴Jones, *Christianity in the Constitution*, 288-338.

¹⁵Jones, *Christianity in the Constitution*, 478-549.

¹⁶Jones, *Christianity in the Constitution*, 550-653.

¹⁷The alternative—permitting all religious groups freedom to do whatever their religions and their diverse or perverse ethical systems permit or command their adherents to do—would destroy national law by permitting people to do *anything* in the name of religious liberty. For the diverse religions of men do have quite various ethical codes and demands, including: human sacrifice; sexual perversion and immorality; cannibalism; the immolation or other means of killing of the wife of a deceased husband; jihads, or holy wars against those who do not believe in the religion; polygamy; and various other violations of the clearly held ethical beliefs of early Americans and their statesmen, including the statesmen who gave us the Constitution and the First Amendment.

¹⁸The evidence below is adapted from Jones, *Christianity in the Constitution*, 662-734.

¹⁹*The Annals of Congress, The Debates and Proceedings in the Congress of the United States*, Vol. I, Compiled from *Authentic Materials* by Joseph Gales, Senior (Washington, D.C.: Gales and Seaton, 1834), 949-950; cited in Gary DeMar, "A Response to Dr. William J. Edgar and the National Confession" (Atlanta: American Vision, 1987), 5.

²⁰Dreisbach, *Real Threat and Mere Shadow*, 67.

²¹Stokes, *Church and State in the United States*, I, 484-486.

²²Charles V. LaFontaine, S.A., "God and the Nation in Selected U.S. Presidential Inaugural Addresses, 1789-1945: Part Two," *Journal of Church and State*, 18, No. 3 (Autumn 1976), 503. See also Part One of the article, *Journal of Church and State*, 18, No. 1 (Winter, 1976), 38-60.

[23]LaFontaine, 503.

[24]LaFontaine, 503.

[25]The fact that some scholars hold that Washington's "Farewell Address" was authored by Alexander Hamilton and then reworked by Washington in no way detracts from the authority of Washington in delivering the address, or from the authority of the address itself. On the contrary, it lends the great authority of Hamilton, one of the most able, prominent, and influential of the Framers of the Constitution, and one of the foremost statesmen of the Federalist era, to the "Farewell Address." And lest it be supposed that Hamilton intended to praise "religion" in general, it should be remembered that this same Alexander Hamilton, in response to the bloody rationalism of the French Revolution, called for the creation of a "Christian Constitutionalist Society."

[26]Milton Lomask, "I do solemnly swear . . ."; The Story of the Presidential Inauguration (New York: Ariel Books, 1966), 7.

[27]The alleged silence of the Constitution concerning God and the Second Person of the Trinity, Jesus Christ, is discussed in Jones, Christianity in the Constitution, 231-287; the issue of the Constitution's recognition and statement of the lordship of Christ is discussed in pages 257-264.

[28]Lomask, 7-10. Coolidge and Arthur, the only other presidents (before Lyndon Johnson) who were first sworn into office under similar circumstances, first took emergency private or semiprivate oaths of office without the Bible, but later participated in public ceremonies in the Capitol in which the Bible was used. Lomask, 7-10.

[29]Nannie McCormick Coleman, The Constitution and Its Framers (Chicago: The Progress Co., 1910), 616-617.

[30]Coleman, 616-617.

[31]Morris, Christian Life and Character of the Civil Institutions of the United States, 560-612, provides evidence of such proclamations at the colony or the state level. Morris, 525-544, provides evidence of such proclamations at the national level and discusses Jefferson's role in the Virginia proclamation mentioned above.

[32]Quoted in Eidsmoe, The Christian Legal Advisor (Grand Rapids: Baker Book House, 1987), 132.

[33]Eidsmoe, The Christian Legal Advisor, 132; Morris, 544-545.

[34]Robert L. Cord, Separation of Church and State: Historical Fact and Current Fiction (New York: Lambeth Press, 1982), 53.

[35]These proclamations are quoted in Morris, 545-550.

[36]Cord, 38-44, 47.

[37]Charles J. Emmerich, "The Enigma of James Madison on Church and State," in Luis E. Lugo, ed., Religion, Public Life, and the American Polity (Knoxville: University of Tennessee Press, 1993), 61-62.

[38]Cord, 17-47.

[39]Emmerich, 60-61.

[40]Morris, Christian Life and Character of the Civil Institutions of the United States, 135-136.

[41]See Daniel L. Dreisbach, "In Pursuit of Religious Freedom: Thomas Jefferson's Church-State Views Revisited," in Lugo, ed., Religion, Public Life, and the American Polity, 74-114.

[42]Cord, 41-45.

[43]Jones, Christianity in the Constitution, 478-549.

[44]See Jones, Christianity in the Constitution, 550-623.

[45]Stokes, Church and State in the United States, 499-504. Doctrinal controversy arose when Roman Catholics appeared in the pulpit, and especially in the early 1820s,

when Unitarians such as the famous Unitarian minister Jared Sparks were invited to preach. Stokes, 501-504.

[46]Stokes, 499-503.

[47]Stokes, 505-506.

[48]Brant, *The Bill of Rights: Its Origin and Meaning*, 417, claims the Treaty with Tripoli as "an official statement of the relationship of the American government to Christianity," but does not inform his readers that there is no such provision in the original treaty; fails to tell his readers that the original, supposed, treaty was modified, in 1805, to remove the offending clause; and "neglects" to cite any of the many other treaties which contain obviously Christian language or statements.

Apparently, for the secularizers, the first—bogus—Tripoli Treaty is more "official" than either the revised treaty or all the other Christian treaties. See Gary DeMar, *America's Christian History: The Untold Story* (Powder Springs, Georgia: American Vision, 2000, Second Edition), 131-144.

[49]For information on the treaties mentioned above, see Cord, *Separation of Church and State*, 57-60.

[50]Cord, 62.

[51]Antieau, Downey and Roberts, *Freedom from Federal Establishment: Formation and Early History of the First Amendment's Religion Clauses*, 167. As these authors note (168-174), state governments also gave aid to Christian education for the same reasons.

[52]Cord, 80.

[53]De Jonge and Van Der Slik, *Separation of Church and State: The Myth Revisited*, 89.

[54]Quoted in De Jonge and Van Der Slik, 89.

[55]Antieau, Downey and Roberts, 188; for a longer quotation from this document, see De Jong and Van Der Slik, 89.

[56]Quoted in De Jonge and Van Der Slik, 89.

[57]Jones, *Christianity in the Constitution*, 79-144.

[58]De Jonge and Van Der Slik, 90.

[59]De Jonge and Van Der Slik, 91-94.

[60]Morris, 613.

[61]Morris, 613.

[62]Quoted in Morris, 615.

[63]Quoted in Morris, 615.

[64]Quoted in Morris, 616.

[65]Quoted in Morris, 618.

[66]Quoted in Morris, 618-619.

[67]Morris, 613, 614, 617.

[68]Bradford, *A Worthy Company*, 122; conversation with the present writer, 1980.

[69]Morris, 620.

[70]Quoted in Morris, 620-621.

[71]Morris, 620.

[72]DeMar, *America's Christian History*, 122, 124-126.

[73]Quoted in Louis M. Kohlmeier, Jr., *"God Save This Honorable Court!"* (New York: Charles Scribner's Sons, 1972), 15.

[74]Isaac Cornelison, *The Relation of Religion to Civil Government in the United States of America*, 144.

[75]Quoted in Morton, 130.

[76]Morton, 130-131.

[77]Quoted in Morton, 131.

[78]Morton, 126.

[79]Quoted in Morton, 133-134, and in Cornelison, 144-145.

[80]Morton, 141-142.

[81]Quoted in the address of Dr. A.A. Miner to the National Convention to Secure the Religious Amendment to the Constitution of the United States, New York, February 26, 1873, in *The Religious Amendment of the Constitution of the United States* (Philadelphia: James B. Rodgers Co., 1875), 29-30. These demands are also discussed in other speeches to the 1873 and 1874 conventions of this organization, and in R.L. Dabney, *Discussions*, Vol. II, *Evangelical* (Harrisonburg, Virginia: Sprinkle Publications, [1891] 1982), 598ff.

About the Author

Archie P. Jones has taught American Government, American Political Thought, Modern Political Thought, Composition, American Literature, and related subjects at Texas A&M University, Grove City College, and some extended campuses of Saint Leo College and Embry-Riddle Aeronautical University. He has also taught Government, U.S. Constitution, and various history courses at two Christian schools and been a field representative for a U.S. Congressman. He currently teaches at Rocky Bayou Christian School in Niceville, Florida, and is an adjunct assistant professor for Embry-Riddle Aeronautical University. He also serves as a consultant and lecturer on America's Christian history for the Plymouth Rock Foundation.

Dr. Jones is the author of dozens of articles and book reviews. His six audio and videotaped *Lectures on the Constitution* are available from the Plymouth Rock Foundation. In addition to *Church and State: The Federal Record,* he is the author of seven other mini-books: *America's First Covenant: Christian Principles in the Articles of Confederation; Christianity and Our State Constitutions, Declarations and Bills of Rights, Parts I and II; Christian Principles in the Constitution and the Bill of Rights, Parts I and II; Thomas Jefferson: The Man and the Myth* (all published by the Plymouth Rock Foundation), and *The Influence of Historic Christianity on Early America* (Chalcedon Foundation).

A Marine Corps veteran, he received his A.B. (cum laude), M.A. and D.C.T. degrees from the University of Miami (Florida) and his Ph.D. in Politics from the University of Dallas. His doctoral dissertation is "Christianity in the Constitution: The Intended Meaning of the Religion Clauses of the Constitution" (University of Dallas, 1991).

Dr. Jones is a member of Trinity Presbyterian Church, Valparaiso, Florida. He and his wife, Mary, and their two children, Daniel and Jennie, reside in Niceville, Florida.

GOD AND GOVERNMENT: ASK THE FOUNDERS

Chief Justice Roy S. Moore

GOD & GOVERNMENT:
ASK THE FOUNDERS

Chief Justice Roy S. Moore

More than five years after the ACLU launched its legal jihad to force prayer and the Ten Commandments from his courtroom, Roy Moore became Chief Justice of the Alabama Supreme Court. Moore, an Alabama circuit court judge who refused to back down when the ACLU charged that prayer and his courtroom plaque bearing the Ten Commandments violated the First Amendment, easily defeated his electoral opponent in November 2000 to become Chief Justice of the state's Supreme Court.

Throughout his campaign, Moore promised to take the Ten Commandments with him should he become Chief Justice. "The Ten Commandments will be publicly displayed at the Alabama Supreme Court, just as they are in many courts across our land," Moore said before he was sworn in as Chief Justice.

And if the ACLU sues, charging as before that such a display violates the Constitution, Moore, a West Point graduate and Vietnam veteran, has promised to "fight them with everything and every ounce of strength I have."

Moore's electoral victory in 2000 capped an unlikely sequence of events that began in 1995, when the ACLU sued, claiming he had violated the Constitution's alleged mandate of a "wall of separation" between church and state. Moore fought back energetically, winning national attention for his unbending and articulate defense of divine acknowledgements in public life. He prevailed against the ACLU after three years, when the Alabama Supreme Court in 1998 threw the case out on technical grounds.

Moore, who vowed he would not remove the Ten Commandments or prayer, regardless of the cost, became a hero to many in Alabama as the lawsuit progressed. A 1997 Judge Moore rally attracted some 25,000 people, and a poll that year found that 88 percent of Alabama residents sided with him. Then-governor Fob James waded into the conflict, declaring that should Moore lose in the courts, he would call out the Alabama National Guard to prevent marshals from removing the Ten

Commandments from Moore's courtroom.

Moore's legal challenges did not end after the ACLU lawsuit was dismissed. Two state bodies looked into allegations of ethical misconduct lodged against Judge Moore, but he was cleared of all charges.

Dr. Kennedy and Coral Ridge Ministries stood by Judge Moore throughout his ordeal, providing more than $130,000 for his legal defense fund. That help proved crucial according to Moore defense attorney Stephen Melchior. "Without it," he said, "we would have been dead in the water years ago."

Chief Justice Moore received the 1997 Christian Statesman of the Year award from the D. James Kennedy Center For Christian Statesmanship. He has been honored with the Family, Faith and Freedom Citation from the Family Research Council and the National Spirit of Life Award from the African American Family Association. Michigan Governor John Engler and the State of Michigan presented him with a special tribute, calling Moore "a great American and an honorable judge."

He has appeared on numerous national television and radio programs, including The Today Show, 20/20, NBC Nightly News, ABC World News, and The Coral Ridge Hour. Articles about him have appeared in USA Today, The Los Angeles Times, The Washington Times, The Washington Post, The Houston Chronicle, The Atlanta Constitution, and elsewhere.

Moore and his wife Kayla have four children, Heather, Roy, Caleb and Micah, and are members of the First Baptist Church of Gallant, Alabama.

The following message was delivered by Chief Justice Moore to Coral Ridge Ministries' 2001 Reclaiming America For Christ Conference, held in Newport Beach, California.

• • • • •

Thank you very much. Well, indeed, it's an honor to be here in beautiful Newport Beach, California. I was so excited about coming here. I got up Thursday morning and was getting everything ready so I wouldn't forget anything, and I forgot something. It was mid-morning before my wife reminded me it was her birthday.

If any of you guys know how much trouble you can get into when you forget your wife's birthday, you'll know what I'm talking about. I had always wanted to take her to a faraway land and give her an exotic dinner and have a lot of guests. Well, California's rather exotic. We had a wonderful meal down by the beach, and if you will, on the count of three, just say "Happy Birthday, Kayla," you'll save me a lot of trouble—1-2-3, "Happy Birthday, Kayla."

Seriously, it's not good to forget your wife's birthday. We men sometimes take things like that for granted. A marriage relationship is very special; and when you begin it, of course, you don't forget your wife's birthday. But as time goes on, we get forgetful and become hard of hearing.

I recall an older couple who were sitting on their front porch in Alabama, rocking back and forth. They'd been married 65 years. The older gentleman looked at his wife, and she hadn't been very friendly all day. It was in the twilight hours, and he suddenly remembered it was her birthday. He hadn't said, "Happy Birthday"; he hadn't bought her flowers. He had no gift, no card. So he thought, well, I'll just lean over and say something sweet to her. Now, she was hard of hearing; and he leaned over and said, "Darling, our love is tried and true."

And she said, "Aye?"

So he said it a little louder. He said, "Darling, our love is tried and true."

And she said, "Huh?"

He said, "Tried and true. Tried and true."

And she said, "I'm tired of you, too."

You know, that's a picture of America today. Haven't we been a little hard of hearing with our pastors, our preachers, and our biblical teachers? Haven't our eyes been closed? Haven't we become forgetful of what God has done for us? Have we not lost our understanding, just like that older couple, which leads to uncomfortable results, to say the least? Jesus said it very simply in Matthew:

> "And in them the prophecy of Isaiah is fulfilled, which
> says: 'Hearing you will hear and shall not understand,

and seeing you will see and not perceive; for the hearts of this people have grown dull. Their ears are hard of hearing, and their eyes they have closed, lest they should see with their eyes and hear with their ears, lest they should understand with their hearts and turn, so that I should heal them'" (Matthew 13:14-15).

Anger Management Not the Answer

I think that we certainly have lost our understanding, an example of which occurred at Santana High School, right here in California. In March of this year, a young man by the name of Andy Williams entered the school and shot two dead and wounded 13—because he had been called names. The solution that many in the education establishment saw was to establish "anti-bullying" programs. In fact, a bill in the Colorado legislature required the implementation of an anti-bullying plan.

In Bloomington, Minnesota, at Kennedy High School, one young man testified that they were giving him tracings of his hand and asking him to take a pledge not to use his hands for violence. There's just one minor problem. According to the AP article in the newspaper, Santana High School had, since 1999 (after Columbine), implemented conflict resolution classes and anger management courses, and they didn't stop the violence. You see, it didn't work there. As it is written in Proverbs 8:1, "Does not wisdom cry out, and understanding lift up her voice?"

The title of that AP article was "The Bully Factor: California Shooting Prompts New Look at an Old Problem." Well, I'll tell you the only thing I agreed with was "New Look at an Old Problem," because it's one of the oldest problems around. When a nation forgets God, it suffers these tragedies.

So I turned to the example of one of those nations. You know, we're not the first. Right in the book of Jeremiah we find the nation of Judah turned from God. They had forgotten God. And so has America perverted its ways and forgotten the Lord God. You see, that's the problem—we're forgetting God. Jeremiah said very clearly,

Right in the book of Jeremiah we find the nation of Judah turned from God. They had forgotten God. And so has America perverted its ways and forgotten the Lord God.

"Hear this now, O foolish people, without understanding, who have eyes and see not, and who have ears and hear not: Do you not fear Me?"

says the Lord. "Will you not tremble at My presence?" (Jeremiah 5:21-22a).

We've forgotten God in this land. But it wasn't always so. Go back with me a few years to June 1944. Now, many of you lived in that time. Many of you remember that America was a very different place then. It wasn't so long ago and there was a war on then. We didn't have TVs. There were no computers, no microwaves. We did have phones, and they were on a party line, so there were no secrets.

But people were very different then. We didn't have drive-by shootings. We didn't have school massacres; abortion was against the law; fathers didn't desert their families; and mothers wanted a father for their child. Material possessions were few. But we did have one thing back then that we seemed to have lost and that is faith in God.

President Franklin D. Roosevelt led the nation in prayer on D-Day, June 6, 1944. AP Photo

Turning to God Before Normandy

I took you back to 1944, specifically June 6, for a particular reason, for it was on that day that Operation Overlord of the Normandy invasion occurred. And as families gathered around their small radio sets, the voice of President Franklin Delano Roosevelt came on the air and asked them to join with him in prayer:

Almighty God, our sons, pride of our nation, this day have set upon a mighty endeavor, a struggle to preserve our Republic, our religion and our civilization, and to set free a suffering humanity.... They will need Thy blessings. Their road will be long and hard.... Some will never return. And for us at home—fathers, mothers, children, wives, sisters and brothers of brave men overseas—whose thoughts and prayers are ever with them—help us, Almighty God, to rededicate ourselves in renewed faith in Thee this hour of great sacrifice.... Give us strength, too.... And, O Lord, give us faith. Give us faith in Thee, faith in our sons, faith in each other, faith in our united crusade. With Thy blessings, we shall prevail over the unholy forces of our enemy.... Thy will be done, Almighty God. Amen.

Our nation turned to God in its darkest hour. The next year, 1945, that war came to an end and so did the life of President Franklin Delano Roosevelt. He was replaced by another man—a man we all know as "Give 'em Hell, Harry"—Harry Truman. He said something in his inaugural address in 1949 that I love to recite. He said,

> The American people stand firm in the faith which has inspired this nation from the beginning. We believe that all men have a right to equal justice under law and equal opportunity to share in the common good. We believe that all men have the right to freedom of thought and expression. We believe that all men are created equal because they are created in the image of God. From this faith we will not be moved.

When Harry Truman left office, the commander of Normandy became president—Dwight David Eisenhower. Together with the Congress, he took steps to insure that the world would never forget that this nation was a nation devoted to Almighty God.

- In 1952, they set aside a day other than Sunday, so that the people could turn to God in prayer—a National Day of Prayer.
- In 1955, by an act of Congress, they put "In God We Trust" on every piece of our money. It had been there before, but not on every piece.
- In 1956 they established a national motto by law—"In God We Trust."
- In 1954 in a joint resolution, in addition to an act of Congress of June 22, 1942, they put "Under God" in the Pledge of Allegiance. They said the inclusion of God in the Pledge would further acknowledge the dependence of our people and our government upon the moral directions of the Creator. By the addition of the phrase "Under God" to the Pledge, the consciousness of the American people will be more alerted to the true meaning of our country and its form of government; but more importantly, so would educators. The children of our land, in the daily recitation of the pledge in school, will be impressed with the true

understanding of our way of life and its origins.

Today we forbid even the mention of God in school. "That's against the First Amendment to the United States Constitution." But Congress addressed that. They said, and I quote:

> It should be pointed out that the adoption of this legislation in no way runs contrary to the provisions of the First Amendment of the Constitution. This is not an act establishing a religion or one interfering with the free exercise of religion. A distinction must be made between the existence of religion as an institution and a belief in the sovereignty of God.

That's where we're failing today. We've forgotten that there's a difference. Have we been moved? Oh, I think we have. God is forbidden in our schools, in our federal workplaces, in our public institutions. Some would say it's the law. Others would say it's prohibited by the Constitution of the United States—a violation of the First Amendment to the United States Constitution. In no way.

God is forbidden in our schools, in our federal workplaces, in our public institutions. Some would say it's the law. Others would say it's prohibited by the Constitution of the United States—a violation of the First Amendment to the United States Constitution. In no way.

I'm Chief Justice of the state of Alabama. I've spoken all over this country. I've spoken to Supreme Court justices of different states. Unfortunately, the lawyers and judges of our land do not know the First Amendment to the United States Constitution. They don't know the Constitution. I'll clarify that a little bit and say that they may know parts of the Constitution, but they certainly don't know the First Amendment. I carry a copy of it around with me because every judge in every state is sworn to uphold this document.

Article 6 says, "This Constitution, and the Laws of the United States which shall be made in Pursuance thereof; and all Treaties made, or which shall be made, under the Authority of the United States, shall be the supreme Law of the Land; and the Judges in every State shall be bound thereby, anything in the Constitution or Laws of any State to the

Contrary notwithstanding." You see, we are supposed to know the Constitution and our Constitution was based on a belief in God.

I took an oath in 1969 when I graduated from the United States Military Academy and prior to going to Vietnam to support and defend the Constitution of the United States. I've taken that oath on several different occasions, and I can tell you that I've always ended that oath with these words, "So help me God," straight out of the Judiciary Act of 1789. None other than George Washington said before the Constitutional Convention that the event was in the hand of God. Oh, there was a big disagreement between them. They knew they were going to have trouble forming a new Constitution.

Someone asked Washington about it. Gouverneur Morris, years later at Washington's death, gave an oration, and in it he repeated Washington's reply: "It is too probable that no plan we propose will be adopted. Perhaps another dreadful conflict is to be sustained. If, to please the people, we offer what we ourselves disapprove, how can we afterwards defend our work? Let us raise a standard to which the wise and the honest can repair. The event is in the hand of God."

James Madison knew about it. He was the chief architect of that Constitution. He took the notes of the convention. In *Federalist No. 43*, which is a document written in the newspapers trying to convince people to convince their legislators and their representatives to adopt this Constitution, he said it was written as if by the finger of God.

In *Federalist No. 43*, he said that some might question the beginning of Article VII of this Constitution: "The Ratification of the Conventions of nine States, shall be sufficient for the Establishment of this Constitution between the States so ratifying the Same."

There it is. God is all over it, or don't you see that? Madison saw it. Because in *Federalist 43* he said that some might wonder how the Confederation formed of 13 states can be done away with by a vote of nine. Seems a little unfair. Well, he asked, quoting here from *Federalist 43*, by what principle can "the Confederation, which stands in the solemn form of a compact among the States, ... be superseded without the unanimous consent of the parties to it?" He was asking how can they do away with what 13 states have done with just nine states?"He answered it in this way:

> The first question is answered at once by recurring to the absolute necessity of the case; to the great principle of self-preservation; to the transcendent law of nature and of

nature's God, which declares that the safety and happiness of society are the objects at which all political institutions aim, and to which all such institutions must be sacrificed.

I think the fourth president of the United States, the chief architect of the Constitution, is good authority that this Constitution exists because of the laws of God; and without the laws of God, we would not have a Constitution. It's absolutely ludicrous to say that that Constitution prohibits an acknowledgment of God.

> ... *this Constitution exists because of the laws of God; and without the laws of God, we would not have a Constitution.*

September 25, 1789, was a very important date. That's the date the first Congress approved the First Amendment. I have the records of the Congress here, and let me tell you what else they did on that very date. Congress "resolved, that a joint committee of both Houses be directed to wait upon the President of the United States and request that he would recommend to the people of the United States a day of public thanksgiving and prayer."

Eight days later Washington issued a proclamation for the first day of prayer: "Whereas it is the duty of all nations to acknowledge the providence of Almighty God, to obey His will, to be grateful for His benefits, and humbly to implore His protection and favor.... Now therefore I do recommend and assign Thursday, the 26th day of November next, to be devoted by the People of these States to the service of that great and glorious Being, who is the beneficent Author of all the good that was, that is, or that will be."

What About Separation of Church and State?

I could go on and on about the different firsts that occurred, but some would say, "What about this separation of church and state? Judge, don't you know about separation of church and state?" Well, it doesn't mean to separate God from our country. Church and God are not synonymous. Besides, you know that the phrase came from a letter Thomas Jefferson wrote on January 1, 1802. Certainly, he didn't mean to separate religion from government, did he? I think not.

I have Manasseh Cutler's diary here. He was a Congressman. Do you know what Jefferson did on January 3, two days later? He was sitting in church, listening to John Leland, the Baptist minister in Congress.

But I don't need Manasseh Cutler's diary, I only need the Declaration of Independence, where Jefferson says that we were entitled to exist by the "Laws of Nature and of Nature's God." See what you get out of these sentences:

> We hold these Truths to be self-evident, that all Men are created equal, that they are endowed by their Creator with certain unalienable Rights, that among these are Life, Liberty and the Pursuit of Happiness—That to secure these Rights, Governments are instituted among Men, deriving their just Powers from the Consent of the Governed, that whenever any Form of Government becomes destructive of these Ends, it is the Right of the People to alter or to abolish it, and to institute new Government, laying its Foundation on such Principles and organizing its Powers in such Form, as to them shall seem most likely to effect their Safety and Happiness.

Now, did he mean to separate God and government, or did he say God gave us our rights? Government is there to secure them, and if it doesn't, it should be abolished.

They say, "But judge, you're not supposed to be talking against the common trend. You know, it's not nice to talk about God and government. You're not supposed to display the Ten Commandments. You're not supposed to have prayer before court. You're not supposed to do these things. It's not nice."

Patrick Henry, standing before a little church in Virginia, March 23, 1775, said something I identify with. He said:

> Should I keep back my opinions at such a time as this for fear of giving offense? I should consider myself guilty of treason … and of an act of disloyalty to the majesty of Heaven, which I revere above all earthly kings. It is natural to man to indulge in illusions of hope. We are apt to shut our eyes against a painful truth and listen to the song of the siren until she transforms us into beasts. Is this the part of wise men engaged in the great and arduous struggle for liberty? Are we disposed to be of the number of those who having eyes, see not; who having ears, hear not.

Well, some of us have been so disposed. We're like those two cows standing in the pasture talking. Oh, I don't know in California if your cows talk; I'll have to check. But in Alabama, our cows frequently have conversations, and it seems there were two in the pasture talking, and one cow said to the other, "Have you heard about the disease going around?"

"No, I hadn't heard anything about such a thing."

He replied, "Sure, there's a terrible disease going around. It makes cows go mad. Why they don't even know who they are."

"I hadn't heard anything about it."

"Well, it's a terrible thing. It's destroying our population."

"No. No."

"Well, you don't seem to be too concerned."

The second cow responded, "Well, why should I? I'm a rabbit," and he started hopping across the field.

You see, we need to stop eating grass like a cow, and we need to stop talking like a cow, but act like a rabbit. We need to stop talking like Christians—going to church, but not acting like one. So what is the solution? What's left to do? How can we correct this problem? How can we take our land back? Well, I turned to the book of Jeremiah to see how God told them they should act. It says:

> Thus saith the LORD of hosts, the God of Israel, "Amend your ways and your doings, and I will cause you to dwell in this place. Trust ye not in lying words, saying, The temple of the LORD, The temple of the LORD, The temple of the LORD, are these. For if ye throughly amend your ways and your doings; if ye throughly execute judgment between a man and his neighbour; if ye oppress not the stranger, the fatherless, and the widow, and shed not innocent blood in this place, neither walk after other gods to your hurt: Then will I cause you to dwell in this place, in the land that I gave to your fathers, for ever and ever.

> "Behold, ye trust in lying words, that cannot profit. Will ye steal, murder, and commit adultery, and swear falsely, and burn incense unto Baal, and walk after other gods whom ye know not; and come and stand before Me in this house, which is called by My name, and say, 'We are delivered to do all these abominations? Is this house, which is called by my name, become a den of robbers in your eyes? Behold, even I have seen it," saith the LORD (Jeremiah 7:3-11, KJV).

You see, we can't fool God. He sees. And you ask, "Well, wherein have we robbed God? In tithes and offerings?" In denying His sovereignty. We've robbed Him because we said, "He's not applicable out there. Keep Him in your church."

You see, today we face another war,
Fought not upon some distant shore,
Nor against an enemy that we can't see,
Yet one as ruthless as can be.
He'll take your life and your children, too,
And say there's nothing that you can do.
He'll make you believe that wrong's right,
'Tis but a sign to stand and fight.
And though we face the wrath of hell,
Against those gates we shall prevail.
In schools and homes across our land,
It's time for us to take a stand.
And when our race on earth is run,
And we've fought the fight and our victory's won.
And through the earth His praise will ring,
When all the heavenly angels sing.
'Twill be enough to see the Son,
And hear Him say, "A job well done.
You kept the faith, so strong and true.
I knew that I could count on you."

Thank you.

Section Four

RECLAIMING THE LOST LEGACY

D. James Kennedy, Ph.D.

RECLAIMING THE LOST LEGACY

D. James Kennedy, Ph.D

After reading the colossal evidence for Christianity's critical role in our nation's infancy, you may well wonder: How have we come so far from the intent of our Founders? On a typical Sunday two centuries ago, we would have found President Jefferson listening intently to the Gospel being preached in the hall of the House of Representatives. Now, the right to pray in public forums has, in some cases, been lost and in others is under attack.

How do we counter this "federal takeover of religion?" How do we regain an atmosphere in our country where people can freely exercise their faith in God without government harassment? There are several steps we must take.

1. Pray for God to "Save the Supreme Court"

First, we must realize that much of the blame for the erosion of our religious freedom must be placed on the marble steps of the Supreme Court. This nation desperately needs God to answer the prayer said before each session of the highest court in our land: "God save the United States and this honorable Court." Truly, we must give due honor and respect to the Supreme Court as the institution God has provided to interpret the law of our land for the establishment of justice and righteousness. As the Scriptures say:

> Let every soul be subject to the governing authorities. For there is no authority except from God, and the authorities that exist are appointed by God. Render therefore to all

their due: taxes to whom taxes are due, customs to whom customs, fear to whom fear, honor to whom honor (Romans 13:1, 7).

Honor all people. Love the brotherhood. Fear God. Honor the king (1 Peter 2:17).

While we hold to these basic biblical tenets, we must at the same time pray as citizens of a nation that is "of the people, by the people, and for the people." The Supreme Court's justices must stand for constitutional truth as it was intended by those who framed our national charter. That is their solemn duty.

Even as we insist on adherence to these principles and intercede for God's intervention in judicial affairs, we must also give Him thanks for times when the Supreme Court has acted in accordance with the Constitution and in defense of religious freedom. For example:

- Ensuring the right of Amish parents to educate their children according to their religious convictions;
- Protecting the right of children of Jehovah's Witnesses not to be forced to act against their conscience in public schools (even though we strongly disagree with their beliefs);
- Protecting the tax-exempt status of religious organizations and churches;
- Allowing the states to reimburse private religious schools for the cost of administering state-required tests; and
- Protecting the right of evangelical Christians to have prayer and Bible studies on college campuses.

Even with these decisions, it would be difficult to make a case that the Court in its current composition is seriously committed to preserving religious liberty. The evidence is not in the individual decisions, but in the overall and often-arrogant tone of the Court's broad view of itself. Specifically, the Court's decision-making process is essentially humanistic and man-centered. Consider that the Court continues to:

- Make itself the final arbitrary authority over matters of religion and the state throughout our nation;
- Reinterpret the meaning of the First Amendment as originally understood;

- Change the Establishment Clause to restrict the free exercise of religion in the public sphere;
- Establish secularism as the official religion of the public school system in its effort to create a "neutral" environment; and
- Adopt a secular view of religion as a fading superstition of the past.

The Court must be saved from humanistic understandings of justice, sin and a view of religion as potentially dangerous to society. If we hope to maintain our religious freedom, we must pray for and support the nomination of justices who will hold to an historical understanding of the First Amendment.

The best way to have justices on the Court committed to interpreting the Constitution according to the Framer's original intent is to elect men and women to the presidency and Senate who believe likewise.

We need to understand how our President and senators view the First Amendment, since they are the ones who will appoint and confirm all Supreme Court justices. The best way to have justices on the Court committed to interpreting the Constitution according to the Framers' original intent is to elect men and women to the presidency and Senate who believe likewise. In time, we could return to our nation the historic understanding and purpose of the First Amendment.

Action Steps

1. Pray specifically the prayer said before each U.S. Supreme Court session: "God save this honorable Court!" Ask God for a mighty move of His Spirit to reorder our Supreme Court so that its decisions honor our Constitution.
2. Lift up each member of the Supreme Court. Visit the Supreme Court's website http://www.supremecourtus.gov/ or the many other resources online for details on the Court's members.
3. Contact the President and your senators to let them know of your support for nominees to the Supreme Court and lower federal courts who will interpret the Constitution in a manner faithful to the Framers' original intent.

2. Stop the Silent Insurrection

Second, we must alert our society to the silent legal insurrection going on in the Western world today. As this book has demonstrated, it is not difficult to understand the thoughts and intentions of the Founders of our nation. Yet secularists choose to ignore these realities to recreate their own vision of society.

How many times have you heard, "You can't legislate morality"? On the surface, the vast majority of Americans would agree with that statement. But if you can't legislate morality, what can you legislate? Immorality? The idea that civil law is "amoral" is a new concept to our nation and culture, yet it has now become deeply ingrained in our thinking.

The fact is ... you cannot legislate anything but morality!

The fact is ... you cannot legislate anything but morality! We have laws against murder because it is immoral to murder; we have laws against stealing because it is immoral to steal; we have laws against rape because it is immoral to rape.

This country's legislative enactments were founded incontrovertibly upon the Christian ethic of the Founding Fathers. Even Thomas Jefferson, the man most often pointed to as being against the Christian faith and a strong advocate of the separation of church and state, recommended in his plans for the state-funded University of Virginia that one of its five departments be for "Theology, and Ecclesiastical History; Law, Municipal and Foreign."[1] This clearly indicates that Jefferson saw the intellectual value in educating students in theology and Church history and would not agree with modern advocates of a strict separation of church and state. This is only one indication that our culture and legislation were based on a broadly Christian morality as revealed in the Word of God.

The need for a higher "divine" law to give legitimacy to civil law has been recognized not only by Moses and the Apostles, but by the classical Greeks and Romans as well. Cicero said:

> I find that it has been the opinion of the wisest men that Law is not a product of human thought, nor is it any enactment of peoples, but something eternal which rules the whole universe by its wisdom in command and prohibition. Thus they have been accustomed to say that Law is the primal and ultimate mind of God.[2]

Yet this divine basis for law has been denied since the Enlightenment, two centuries ago. For the last four decades, a view of law as only the whim of man, rather than the reflection of divine justice, has made major inroads into our society and the Supreme Court. Increasingly, in place of this "higher law," we find subjective humanist ethics. When that substitution is complete, we will be living in a very different America.

Abortion, infanticide, homosexuality, divorce, euthanasia, gambling, pornography and suicide are simply a portion of the agenda of secular humanists. That agenda extends to the total removal of every public vestige of Christian faith.

Some humanists even suggest that exposing children to the idea of God may harm their growth and keep them from psychological "balance"; the state therefore should do what it can to keep children from being confronted with the issue of God until they have reached adulthood. That is the logical conclusion of the secularists, and they are imposing this anti-God philosophy under the false teaching that the government is supposed to be neutral concerning God.

In 1851, Daniel Webster made it clear that neutrality toward religion and Christianity was not in the minds of those who fought the Revolution or wrote the Constitution:

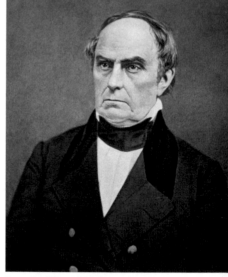

> Lastly, our ancestors established their system of government on morality and religious sentiment. Moral habits, they believed, cannot safely be trusted on any other foundation than religious principle, nor any government be secure which is not supported by moral habits. Living under the heavenly light of revelation, they hoped to find all the social dispositions, all the duties which men owe to each other and to society, enforced and performed. Whatever makes men good Christians, makes them good citizens.[3]

Portrait of Daniel Webster (1782-1852)
Photograph by Mathew B. Brady. © CORBIS

Our Founders never intended for this nation to be secular or anti-God. As Dr. Jones has so well demonstrated, they did not hesitate to call upon God or mention Him in their public utterances or in their public buildings. Nor did they hesitate to offer thanksgiving to Him for His goodness and providence, to set aside special days of praise and prayer and thanksgiving to God, or to establish chaplaincies for the Senate, House of Representatives, and the armed services.

Yet, in a nation such as this, in *Stone v. Graham* (1980), the Supreme Court ruled that Kentucky cannot require the Ten Commandments to be put on the walls of the schools—even though the Commandments are carved in stone on the walls of the Supreme Court building!

Neutrality is a myth. As the concept is now practiced in our public schools, it really establishes secularism as the official religion of the state. It bars teachers and school administrations from mentioning religion, fearing they may breach some "wall of separation" and face a lawsuit from a disgruntled parent. "Neutrality" has established secularism and restricted the free exercise of religion for thousands of American school children and teachers. This concept, rather than ensuring freedom of religion, tyrannizes religion and should be repudiated.

Action Steps

1. Understand the well-documented, but widely unknown historical impact of Christian belief on our nation. For eye-opening additional resources, go to the Library of Congress web site at http://lcweb.loc.gov/exhibits/religion.

2. Access Internet tools (such as those provided by the Center for Reclaiming America) which will give you instant influence at our government's highest levels. Already, Coral Ridge Ministries has forwarded more than 270,000 petitions urging the Supreme Court to practice proper First Amendment jurisprudence. Another 41,000 petitions have been sent to the President urging him to nominate men and women to the federal bench who will practice judicial restraint.

3. Be vigilant in your children's and grandchildren's schools to ensure that our young people are being taught the truth of our nation's history and how that history plays out in modern society. If textbooks and teachers fail to tell the complete truth, remember that the best education is found in the meaningful discussions you have in your own home.

3. Refuse to Be Silenced

Third, we must stand against the efforts of some to exclude Christian believers from public debate on the place of religion in society. The expansion of the Establishment Clause, if taken to its logical conclusion, will move us irresistibly toward the view of separation of church and state held by the now defunct Soviet Union. That view goes like this: The Church is free to do anything the government is not engaged in—but the government is engaged in almost everything! Therefore, the Church is free to stay within its four walls, pray and sing hymns. But anything else will bring swift punishment.

That is what is happening in America. Unfortunately, many churches, pastors and Christians are accepting it, even defending it—saying the Church should not involve itself in politics and other "unspiritual" issues of the day. Ours is, unfortunately, a "politicized" culture in which almost every aspect of life is thought to fall under the aegis of politics. Moral questions—such as abortion, homosexuality, suicide, and so forth—are increasingly the province of the state, not the Church.

The push to silence the voice of faith applies not just to the Church but to individual Christians, as well. As I mentioned in the Introduction, Attorney General John Ashcroft came under attack for his faith, not only during his nomination, but after he took office. When Attorney General Ashcroft continued his longstanding practice of hosting voluntary prayer meetings, the anti-faith elites were up in arms, calling on him to stop violating the so-called "separation of church and state."

The original intent of the First Amendment was not to restrict anyone's religious activities. It was to stop the government from establishing a national church or interfering with the free exercise of one's religion. The Establishment Clause was not a limit on the Free Exercise Clause, but a further expression of how government was to assure religious liberty. We need to return to this historical and objective interpretation of the First Amendment.

Action Steps

1. Be on guard for specific governmental opinions and actions which make the Establishment Clause an instrument of exclusion, rather than an avenue for inclusion.

2. Be unashamed of the Gospel as you exercise your rights. It's true that the Supreme Court has significantly diminished many of our religious liberties. But it's also true that you have rights which are independently and separately religious and political. It is time for Christians to take a stand for their faith in the public forums of our land.

Vote for men and women of strong Christian convictions to serve in political office.

3. Exercise your citizenship by voting for leaders committed to true freedom. It is our duty to select leaders who will honor the Constitution. In fact, I would go one step further: Vote for men and women of strong Christian convictions to serve in political office. As John Jay, our nation's first Chief Justice of the U.S. Supreme Court, said, "It is the duty ... of our Christian nation to select and prefer Christians for their rulers." So be bold in your participation in the electoral process. Don't let the religious bigots intimidate you into silence.

John Jay (1745-1829), American jurist and statesman. Full length portrait, painting by Trumbell. © Bettmann/CORBIS

4. Support Those on the Frontlines

The Church must support those organizations that are standing in the gap, defending our sacred liberties in the courtrooms of America.

One such organization is the Alliance Defense Fund (ADF). ADF was formed in 1994 as a nonprofit organization committed to the advocacy of religious freedom, the sanctity of life, and family values. ADF pursues its mission by coordinating the legal efforts of attorneys working on cases in support of its three-fold purpose of: advocacy, providing training for current and future Christian attorneys, and funding cases that have the potential to set favorable precedents.

Alliance Defense Fund was founded by this author, Bill Bright, Larry Burkett, James Dobson, Marlin Maddoux, Don Wildmon and William Pew in order to consolidate resources and build a formidable counter to groups like the American Civil Liberties Union. Since its inception, ADF has profoundly impacted the American legal system through an aggressive application of its mission. All of the key post-1994 Supreme Court cases mentioned in this book were ADF-backed cases. Coral Ridge Ministries is pleased to be able to financially support the Alliance Defense Fund and to offer continued support and counsel through its national board.

Action Steps

1. Be aware of judicial issues in our nation and in your own community. Dig deeper than what you might see on the evening

news or in the headlines. Research the issues for yourself and be able to converse intelligently about these matters. Resources such as www.reclaimamerica.org are available to provide research assistance.
2. Become familiar with the Alliance Defense Fund, especially when religious liberties are being threatened in your own community. The toll-free telephone number is (800) TELL-ADF and the address is: 8960 Raintree Drive, Suite 300, Scottsdale, AZ 85260. You may also access ADF on the Internet at www.alliancedefensefund.org.

Reclaiming the Lost Legacy

Unfortunately, instead of taking an active role in the cause of religious liberty, many American Christians choose to do nothing. Why? Maybe they are not aware of the historical facts that you have been reading. Maybe they are afraid—afraid of the controversy. Perhaps they have forgotten the words of Scripture: "Fear not."

We must have courage. We must take action. The secular humanists have declared war on Christianity in this country, and at the moment they are winning the war. Under the pretext of religious liberty, we who reject this secular philosophy have been forced out of the public arena and onto the sidelines. Even then, the allowable circles of influence are ever-shrinking, as more and more areas of life are "politicized" and made "off-limits" to religion. The First Amendment was meant to limit government, not Christianity, religion or faith.

Why, as Christians, should we be concerned about such issues? Why should we care how the Supreme Court rules on issues of religious freedom? Even if the law were not on our side (but it is!), must we not speak out about our faith?

We must be concerned, because after a society has been secularized, after our children have been forced by law to spend most of their educational lives in an environment that treats God as a non-issue, after every law, every textbook used in public schools, every public celebration, and every monument has been stripped of mention of the Divine, we will find it extremely difficult to speak with people in a meaningful manner about the importance of God and Jesus Christ.

Too extreme to believe? Who would have thought 40 years ago that our young people would no longer be able to pray in our schools? Who would have thought 10 years ago that the Ten Commandments would be shunned in our courthouses? What's next? And who will stand to stop the secular insurrection?

Who would have thought 40 years ago that our young people would no longer be able to pray in our schools?

As Christians, we should strive to see that our society and its institutions conform to His truth and be dedicated to His glory. We should desire that our children's education be directed by a Christian philosophy of life and our Republic transformed by people in covenant relationship with God, living under His rule and law.

The First Amendment, with its prohibition of a federal establishment of religion and endorsement of government's clear duty to promote the free exercise of religion, should create an atmosphere conducive to the free proclamation of the Gospel. Where different views are circulated without government interference, censorship or prejudice, then truth, by God's grace, will be victorious; and Christ will be seen as Savior and Lord.

Let us, therefore, stand firmly behind the historical, objective understanding of the First Amendment and resist all further attempts by the Court to impose the religion of secularism in our public schools … or anywhere else. Let us steadfastly seek a government that allows people to freely exercise their faith in all areas of life—both public and private. And let us labor while there is still time to reclaim the lost legacy of religious liberty that was set out so clearly in our Constitution and given to us as a sacred trust to preserve for generations to come. May God bless these United States of America.

Notes

1. Robert L. Cord, *Separation of Church and State*, (New York: Lambeth Press, 1982), p. 140.
2. Verna M. Hall, *The Christian History of the Constitution of the United States of America* (San Francisco: Foundation for Christian Education, 1966), p. 247.
3. John Warwick Montgomery, *The Law Above the Law* (Minneapolis: Bethany House Publishers, 1975), p. 37.

KEY FIRST AMENDMENT SUPREME COURT RULINGS

KEY FIRST AMENDMENT
SUPREME COURT RULINGS

Meaning and Application of First Amendment

1940 *Cantwell v. Connecticut*—Free exercise clause extended to the states.

1947 *Everson v. Board of Education of Ewing Township*—Establishment clause extended to states, interpreted to mean that government is prohibited from aiding all religions.

1971 *Lemon v. Kurtzman*—Burger's three-part establishment clause test.

Government Rights and Restrictions

1961 *Braunfeld v. Brown, Gallagher v. Crown Kosher Super Market, and McGowan v. State of Maryland* — State may enforce Sabbath observance laws even against persons who observe a different Sabbath.

1970 *Walz v. Tax Commission of the City of New York*—Tax-exempt status of church property upheld.

1972 *Anderson v. Laird*—Compulsory chapel at military academies held unconstitutional.

1978 *McDaniel v. Paty*—State constitutional provision disqualifying clergymen from being legislators struck down.

1982 *Larkin v. Grenel's Den*—State may not give a church veto power over granting of liquor licenses to businesses.

1983 *Marsh v. Chambers*—State legislature may hire clergyman to open sessions with prayer.

1984 *Donnelly v. Lynch*—City may display nativity scene at Christmas.

1987 *Amos v. Corporation of the Presiding Bishop of the Church of Jesus Christ of Latter-Day Saints*—Religious organizations may discriminate in all hiring decisions on religious grounds.

1988 *Bowen v. Kendrick*—Federal funding for faith-based counseling centers that promote teen chastity is constitutional.

1988 *County of Allegheny v. Greater Pittsburgh ACLU*—Disallowed practice of displaying nativity scene; upheld practice of displaying Menorah as part of a holiday display.

1993 *Lamb's Chapel v. Center Moriches Union Free School District*—Struck down as viewpoint discrimination a public school policy that denied use of facilities to a church.

1995 *Rosenberger v. Rector & Visitors*—A public university must distribute funds to Christian publication on equal terms with secular publications.

Individual Rights and Restrictions

1940 *Minersville School District v. Gobitis*—Compulsory Pledge of Allegiance upheld.

1943 *West Virginia State Board of Education v. Barnette*—Compulsory Pledge of Allegiance voided.

1944 *United States v. Ballard*—Faith healer required to prove sincerity of claims, but not validity.

1972 *Wisconsin v. Yoder*—Amish may take children out of school at age 14, despite state statute requiring attendance until age 16.

1981 *Thomas v. Review Board of Indiana Employment Security Division*—State may not deny unemployment benefits to person who quits job for religious reasons.

1982 *Valley Forge Christian College v. Americans United for Separation of Church and State*—Persons lacking personal stake in case have no standing to sue.

1987 *Board of Airport Commissioners v. Jews for Jesus*—Airport is a "public forum," so people may exercise First Amendment freedom of speech and religious rights.

Public School Rights and Restrictions

1948 *McCollum v. Board of Education*—Religious instruction may not be given on public school premises.

1952 *Zorach v. Clauson*—Public school children may be released from classes to attend religious instruction off the premises.

1962 *Engel v. Vitale*—"Regents' prayer" case; authorities may not compose official prayer to be said in public schools.

1963 *School District of Abington Township v. Schempp*—Bible selections read in public schools are devotional exercise and unconstitutional.

1968 *Epperson v. Arkansas*—Law prohibiting teaching of evolution held unconstitutional.

1980 *Stone v. Graham*—State may not require display of the Ten Commandments in public schools.

1981 *Widmar v. Vincent*—Students at public university must be allowed to use facilities for religious purposes.

1987 *Edwards v. Aguillard*—State law requiring balanced treatment of creation science and evolution ruled unconstitutional because of an unconstitutional legislative purpose.

1990 *Westside Board of Education v. Mergens*—Upheld Equal Access Act in secondary schools.

1992 *Lee v. Weisman*—Clergy may not offer prayers during public school graduation ceremonies.

1992 *Zobrest v. Catalina Foothills School District*—Providing interpreter does not violate Establishment Clause.

2000 *Doe v. Santa Fe Independent School District*—Student-initiated, student-led prayer at football games is unconstitutional.

Private School Rights and Restrictions

1925 *Pierce v. Society of the Sisters of the Holy Names of Jesus and Mary*—Parents have constitutional rights to send their children to private schools.

1968 *Board of Education v. Allen*—State may loan textbooks to pupils attending parochial schools.

1973 *Committee for Public Education v. Nyquist*—State aid to parochial schools held unconstitutional.

1973 *Levitt v. Committee for Public Education*—State aid to parochial schools held unconstitutional.

1975 *Meek v. Pettinger*—State aid to parochial schools strictly limited.

1976 *Roemer v. Board of Public Works of Maryland*—State aid to sectarian colleges permitted.

1977 *Wolman v. Walter*—State aid to parochial school limited.

1980 *Committee for Public Education v. Regan*—State aid to parochial schools upheld.

1983 *Mueller v. Allen*—State tax deductions for parochial school tuition upheld.

1983 *Bob Jones University v. United States*—Government may penalize a religious institution for sincerely held beliefs by revoking its tax-exempt status in the interest of public policy.

1997 *Agostini v. Felton*—Public employees may deliver remedial educational services on the parochial school campus.

2000 *Mitchell v. Helms*—Upheld Federal Act providing library books and educational equipment to religious K-12 schools.